TO: BRIAN T. BROOKINS,
THANKS FOR YOUR SUPPORT. BB GOIFIED
IN READING,

IN KINGDOM SERVICE,

Rev. Dr. Jay A. Brookins
2/27/10

IT'S ALL ABOUT THE KINGDOM, VOLUME ONE

IT'S ALL ABOUT THE KINGDOM, VOLUME ONE

10 Sermons with Kingdom Themes

REV. DR. LARRY A. BROOKINS

FOREWORD BY: Dr. C.L. Brookins
AFTERWORD BY: Dr. Clay Evans

authorHOUSE®

AuthorHouse™
1663 Liberty Drive
Bloomington, IN 47403
www.authorhouse.com
Phone: 1-800-839-8640

First published by AuthorHouse 1/21/2010

ISBN: 978-1-4490-6154-8 (e)
ISBN: 978-1-4490-6152-4 (sc)
ISBN: 978-1-4490-6153-1 (hc)

Library of Congress Control Number: 2010900768

Printed in the United States of America
Bloomington, Indiana

This book is printed on acid-free paper.

Scripture quotations used in this book are from the King James and
New International Versions, unless otherwise stated.

Shalom Church Cover Imagery: By permission, "Images © FaithClipart.com
Worship Word Art, Psalms 19:14 Imagery: By permission, "Images © FaithClipart.com

In Dedication:

To my truly supportive parents: Dr. C.L. & Mary F. Brookins—you've encouraged me to pursue all that I am gifted to do and I'm grateful. Thank you for introducing me to God through His Son Jesus Christ, and thank you for being a godly example of love, compassion, sacrifice, and encouragement. Whatever I do and wherever I go, you both shall always be in my heart and a very integral part of my life and endeavors.

In Kingdom Service with Love from # 6 of 8,

Larry A.

In Memory of:

Herbert L. Brookins, Sr.
(April 24, 1955 – July 3, 2004)

"Love Was In His Hands"
By
Charlotte M. Brookins – Hudson
(July 8, 2004)

Herbert Lee Brookins was a wonderful man, who loved to work with his talented hands.
For over 40 years he played the piano and organ, inspired by God, as a self-taught man.
He could listen to music with the sharpest ear, and he wrote notes as they would appear.
He used the gift of love that was in his hands, to bring peace, joy, and love to all in this land.
His hands worked with cars, paint, hammers, nails & wood, & all he touched turned out good.
A rod in his hand captured many a fish that generally ended up in a loved one's dish.
He loved fishing with his Uncle Earl, who thought of Herbert as one of the rarest pearls.
No task asked of him was too large or small; as gifted as Herbert was, he could do it all.
Construction, auto repair, carpentry, painting, and cleaning,
He was a servant, a son, a brother, father and above all things, a friend.
This ode is to my brother, who was a great man; he did all he could with the love in his hands.
He fulfilled his life's purpose as well as anyone can; Praise the Lord, Herbert now rests.
His hands are now in God's Hands.

Much love, your brother – Larry

Table of Contents

FOREWORD

When I was asked to write a foreword for this book I was very elated by the invitation of its author, my third son of four and sixth of eight children, who is also my successor in ministry and now one I proudly call "Pastor."

I can say without bias that Rev. Dr. Larry A. Brookins is very qualified to write this book. He is articulate, gifted, knowledgeable in Scripture, and well-trained in ministry. It contains some of his very fine sermons on the "Kingdom," which were all written and preached by him, and I thank God I've had the opportunity to sit back and say *"that's my boy!"* God could not have given me a more beloved and effective son.

When Dr. Brookins was just a lad he was unusual with his gifts. He was always trying to attain a higher education and gain more knowledge to better service this generation of people. One of his favorite sayings echoes the lyrics of a Charley Wesley hymn: *"A charge to keep I have, a God to glorify, a never-dying soul to save, to be fitted for the sky. To serve this present age, my calling to fulfill; O may it all my powers engaged, to do my Master's Will."* His messages are very inspiring and he preaches with a great deal of clarity.

I am so honored to be his biological father. The church, True Foundation Transformation, has a teaching ministry that has surpassed nationwide teaching ministries and a weekly television outreach that can be viewed and heard in the Chicagoland area each Wednesday night (9:30 PM CST) and Thursday mornings (11:30 AM CST, Chicago Cable TV Channel 36).

Rev. Dr. Brookins has invested his life to teaching and is in demand with his ability to both teach and preach God's Word. This book contains some of his sermons in his extensive *Kingdom* series of sermons, and I know they will bless you as they have me and the congregation of True Foundation Transformation Church.

Dr. Brookins is a man of vision and his message explains while his life demonstrates what he believes and who he believes in. I know because I observe it, and he illustrates, in his rapport with his children that the parent-child relationship is central in Christianity.

These *Kingdom* messages have much high protein content that will enable the seeking and sincere Christian to grow, however; one must read each sermon prayerfully, with an open mind and teachable spirit in order to acquire their truest meanings and value. Far too often, we have forgotten the truth that God not only wants us to experience a change in our outward behavior but also in our inner lives as well. In fact, without inward transformation there can be no lasting outward hope. With this Dr. Brookins believes in Romans 12:1-2: *"I beseech you therefore brethren, by the mercies of God that ye present your bodies a living sacrifice holy, acceptable unto God, which is your reasonable eservice. And be not conformed to this world, but be ye <u>transformed</u> by the renewing of your mind that ye may prove what is that good, and acceptable, and perfect Will of God."*

Dr. Larry A. Brookins is committed to Biblical principles, the Lordship of Jesus Christ and a Spirit filled life of purpose and servanthood. He possesses a gift for friendship and inspires great allegiance and affection with others and from others. Yes indeed, Dr. Brookins is very humble and genuinely anxious to know more about Christ so that he can make Christ better known to others. For those people who see and hear him cannot honestly fail to see and hear that he is a man of God, sent by God, and whose hallmark is his monumental modesty, sympathy and empathy with human needs that spring from his walk with God. I am sure that once you read these messages about the *Kingdom*, you will want to pass them on and read them again. They contain essential and urgent word for this generation, as well as future generations. It is a collection of messages needs to be heard and heeded if Christians are to become the real *"salt of the earth"* and *"light of the world"* that we are commanded and expected by God to be, and I highly recommend it also for self-edification.

Finally, what God has done and is doing with and through Rev. Dr. Larry A. Brookins is amazing. His sermons are profound and yet simple; so simple that even young people of our congregation both listen and take notes. I often see them sharing their notes with him after service. These are truly sermons for the 21st Century Church that both the young and old can connect with and learn from. As you read each sermon and meditate on its theme, thought, and communication, my prayer is that you will be blessed and more confident having read that there is more to church than simply 'going to church;' as his title projects: *"It's all about the Kingdom!"* Let the 'Word' be the WORD and be faithful to the *Kingdom*, as well as to our Lord and Savior Jesus Christ, until He comes again.

Dr. C.L. Brookins

Founder & Pastor-Emeritus, True Foundation Transformation Church

INTRODUCTION

As long as I can remember I've been a part of the church, not necessarily the Body of Christ, but a part of a people who gathered together on Sundays to have what we called — "church." At the age of twelve I professed a personal faith in Jesus Christ, accepting Him as my Savior, but not necessarily as my Lord. It was something that we were compelled and expected to do, as well as strongly urged to do as children of a preacher. And I do not despise my decision, for over time I've come to appreciate the magnitude of my choice and to enjoy the place and position I now have in the *Kingdom*. It is truly about *The Kingdom!* Oh that Christians would embrace the *Kingdom!*

When I initially preached one message entitled *"Kingdom Commitment"* on February 10, 2008, I never thought that the one would become a year-long plus series of sermons gripped in *Kingdom* themes and riveted with *Kingdom* perspectives. I also never imagined the scope of what God had begun to birth in our spirit and awake in my mind, as 'Kingdom Commitment' gave way to this volume of 10 sermons, which is only Volume One of many more yet to be printed.

In all honesty, this book is the byproduct of an appeal from my father, Dr. C.L. Brookins, who week by week, as I preached each sermon approached me with the vision to put into print the manuscripts of each message. He pressed upon me a sense of urgency not to procrastinate or defer in taking upon myself this endeavor of further witness and spiritual illumination on the theme of the *Kingdom*.

As I've undertaken this task, I now realize the purpose in so doing and I thank my father for seeing in me what God is doing through me—

something he considers worthy of the publication of this volume and others. I above all 'thank God,' who impressed upon me to make clear that in all things, *"It's all about the Kingdom!"*

Throughout the teachings of Jesus the *Kingdom* is central. As a matter of fact, as He commenced His ministry following His baptism in the Jordan River, temptation in the wilderness, and the imprisonment of John the Baptist, Jesus began to preach and resound the very message of John: **"Repent, for the Kingdom of Heaven is at hand"** (Matt 4:17). This message, with a focus on sin remorse, also highlights the present reality of the *Kingdom* as the rule of God in the human heart. It is here, the human heart, where God is received, and it is here, the human heart, where God is obeyed. In this, we say as Jesus taught us to say, **"Thy Kingdom come"** and **"Thy will be done"** (Matt 6:10).

As presented to us by Christ the *Kingdom* has something to do with how we live in our contemporary culture, space, and place, and everything to do with the practical affairs of daily life. To become a part of the *Kingdom* is to undergo a metamorphosis of mindset, lifestyle, speech, and purpose. It is a transformation of values, priorities, short-term goals and lifelong missions in favor of God's Will for our lives. As citizens, we are commanded to represent and reflect the spirit of the *Kingdom* in all we do, think and say. The *Kingdom* is present and future, and we advance the 'Kingdom agenda' as we flesh out the Gospel message throughout the entire world and exalt its King as Savior and Lord.

As *new creations in Christ*, we are to *"seek first the Kingdom"* way, make the *Kingdom* agenda a priority within our lives, govern ourselves by *Kingdom* decree, and as a part of the Church, to be an expression of the *Kingdom* during our sojourn here on earth. Is the Church the *Kingdom*? The answer is "no;" however, God *in Christ* established the Church to manifest the *Kingdom* here on earth. The Church is also God's agent for the establishment of the *Kingdom*. Her *message* is preached through the Church. Her *light* is seen through the Church. Her *words* are heard through the Church, and her *growth* depends upon the efforts of the Church. I say *her* in referring to the Church because the Church is seen to be, in Scripture, *the bride of Christ*. You know God endows the female species with the ability to reproduce and as such, the Church should be birthing new life into the Kingdom.

The Church is the community of the *Kingdom* here on earth, and it is God's desire to reveal His *Kingdom* through the Church. Therefore, it is critical for the Church, not a building or place, but a people with

Kingdom purpose, passion, and priority to exemplify the *Kingdom* through our commitment to the *Kingdom*, and our focus on the *Kingdom*, and our investments in the *Kingdom*, and through our attitudes, characteristics, servanthood and life intent. Understand that for Jesus, the *Kingdom* was His main concern, and His life, ministry, daily words, and even His death attest to its importance and principal position within His life, which cannot ever be overlooked and understated. As disciples of Christ, we are encouraged to walk in the footsteps of Jesus (1 Peter 2:21 & 1 John 2:6) and to take on the very mindset of Christ (Philippians 2:5). In this, we are called *"Christians,"* and in this, we showcase to the world from generation to generation that *"It's all about the Kingdom!"*

Allow the manuscripts of these ten *Kingdom* sermons to speak, enlighten, and equip you. Let the very words, which the Holy Spirit conveyed to me illumine within you, as well as pull out of you a great or greater zeal to be an embodiment of the *Kingdom's* commitment, greatness, priorities, investments, focus, economics, purpose, attitudes, characteristics, and privilege. I so pray that each sermon will inspire as they are read—as they inspired as they were preached.

IN KINGDOM SERVICE,

Rev. Dr. Larry A. Brookins

Footnote: *I've inserted Scripture references where Scripture quotations are pronounced so that you may search the Word for yourself in validation of what is declared.*

ACKNOWLEDGMENT

Wife
Sandra D. Brookins

Children
Tony L. (Kendra)
Larry A. II
Jordan I.

Grandchildren
Jasmine L.
Aleah L.M.
Jayden L.

Siblings
Patricia A. (Huey)
Clara D. (Robert)
Charlotte M. (Greg)
Clarence L. (Ann)
Herbert L. (deceased)
Faye D. (Leroy)
Danny D.K.

Father and Mother-in-Law
Percy L. and Venette Davis

<u>Supportive Friends</u>
Dr. Norman E. and Karen Hutchins
Rev. Dr. Richard and Ingrid Bishop
Evangelist Lemmie Battles
Rev. Dr. Kent Poindexter
Gregory and Deborah Pamon

<u>Giving Honor</u>
Dr. Clay Evans
Dr. Benjamin Garrett
Rev. Lacy J. Banks

<u>Special Thanks</u>
Renee K. Robinson
Attorney Tracie R. Porter
Tomeka M. Owens

<u>In Remembrance</u>
Rev. Sam and Alafair Scales (maternal grandparents)
Clarence Brookins and Della Burns (paternal grandparents)
Pastor Donnell Horn
Pastor Joseph L. Evans

<u>Congratulations</u>
Barack H. Obama (1st African American U.S. President)

<u>Utmost Praise</u>
God the Father

<u>Utmost Gratitude</u>
Jesus Christ, my Lord and Savior

<u>In Submission to the Guidance of</u>
The Holy Spirit

"Kingdom of God"

The "Kingdom of God" is the rule of an eternal sovereign God over all creatures and things (Psalm 103:19; Daniel 4:3). The "Kingdom of God" is also the designation for the sphere of salvation entered into at the new birth (John 3:5-7), and is synonymous with the "Kingdom of Heaven."

The "Kingdom of God" embraces all created intelligence, both in Heaven and earth that are willingly subject to the Lord and are in fellowship with Him. The "Kingdom of God" is, therefore, universal in that it includes created angels and mankind. It is eternal, as God is eternal, and it is spiritual – found within all born-again believers. We enter the "Kingdom of God" when we are born again through our acknowledgment and acceptance of Jesus as Savior and Lord, and we are then part of that "Kingdom" for eternity. It is a relationship "born of the spirit" (John 3:5), and we have confident assurance that it is so because the Holy Spirit bears witness with our spirits (Romans 8:16).

God is sovereign, omnipotent, omniscient and the ruler over all of His creation. However, the designation "Kingdom of God" compasses that realm which is subject to God and will be for eternity. The rest of creation will be destroyed. Only that which is part of the "Kingdom of God" will remain.

*Blessed is the man that walketh not in the counsel of the ungodly, nor standeth in the way of sinners, nor sitteth in the seat of the scornful. But his delight is in the law of the LORD; and in His law doth he meditate day and night. And he shall be like a tree planted by the rivers of water, that bringeth forth his fruit in his season; his leaf also shall not wither; and whatsoever he doeth shall prosper. The ungodly are not so: but are like the chaff which the wind driveth away. Therefore the ungodly shall not stand in the judgment, nor sinners in the congregation of the righteous. **For the LORD knoweth the way of the righteous: but the way of the ungodly shall perish.***

Let the **words** of my mouth, and the **meditation** of my heart, be acceptable in thy sight, O Lord, my strength, and my redeemer.

Psalm 19:14

"As ye go, preach, saying, The Kingdom of Heaven is at hand."
(Matthew 10:17)

"SEEK YE FIRST THE KINGDOM OF GOD"
(MATTHEW 6:33)

Jesus of Nazareth

CHAPTER 1: SERMON ONE

KINGDOM COMMITMENT

(FIRST PREACHED - TRUE FOUNDATION TRANSFORMATION CHURCH – 2/10/08)

LUKE 9:57-62
(NIV)

"As they were walking along the road, a man said to Him, "I will follow you wherever you go." (58) Jesus replied, "Foxes have holes and birds of the air have nests, but the Son of Man has no place to lay His head." (59) He said to another man, "Follow Me." But the man replied, "Lord, first let me go and bury my father." (60) Jesus said to him, "Let the dead bury their own dead, but you go and proclaim the Kingdom of God." (61) Still another said, "I will follow you, Lord; but first let me go back and say good-by to my family." (62) Jesus replied, "No one who puts his hand to the plow and looks back is fit for service in the Kingdom of God.""

One of the greatest needs within our homes, and on many jobs, and in relationships, and in most churches is the need for *commitment*. The day in which we live is unlike the days of our parents and grandparents, who endured much and yet hung in there. These are they who remained committed to their families, and committed to their communities, and committed to their churches, and committed to their God. Yet ours is a day of running away from commitment, shunning responsibilities,

1

avoiding duties and of giving up too soon. In these days, when the going gets tough and rough, we look for a way out, instead of looking for a way through, and the term *"commitment"* has become an unwelcomed word. It is somewhat of a dirty word, especially in regards to marriage and ministry.

Nowadays, people would rather shack up or live together, instead of saying *"I do" "till death we do part."* And in the church, the words of Jesus still ring true: **"The harvest is truly great, but the laborers are few"** (Matthew 9:37). And the reason there is lack in the church and lack in terms of Kingdom duty is because of an unwilling among the people of the church and Kingdom to commit. We'd rather sit on the sidelines and watch everyone else struggle to accomplish things that would be so much easier to achieve, if we would only volunteer and commit ourselves to the areas of void and minority within the church.

The text before us is unmistakable in presenting to us the perspective of the Kingdom in regards to discipleship, or as it relates to being a follower of Jesus. Clearly it conveys to us the sentiments of Christ for individuals, who fail to make priority the Kingdom agenda, and for individuals, who make 'excuse' when called upon to make commitment to the Kingdom, or for individuals, who renege on their verbal promises of loyalty and faithfulness and of their devotion to the cause of the Kingdom.

In contrast to the assumption of many that Jesus would never dare to judge us for looking after our family, working overtime to make ends meet, wanting some time to relax or to chill with the spouse and kids; build careers, chase the wealth, and to take care of things that matters most to us, our text and many other teachings of Jesus challenges these theories of a Jesus, who is indifferent about our relationship to Him and unresponsive concerning our commitment to the Kingdom.

As we see in our text, Jesus insists that nothing and that no one is to take priority over following Him, or that spiritual matters outweigh the carnal matters of this world. In other words, taking time out to relax, or taking time out to chill with the spouse and kids, or taking time out to look after the affairs and welfare of family members, and the building of careers, and the chasing of wealth, or working hard to make ends meet are all commendable and perfectly okay, so long as they and all things we do for ourselves are not done at the expense of Kingdom requirement or at the detriment of Kingdom commitment. In such cases, Jesus has a word of Kingdom service disqualification and of Kingdom disapproval, when we 'seek first the things of this world' and when we place low priority in this world on the things of the Kingdom for us to do while we are in this world. In such case, Jesus says, **"No one who puts his hand to the plow and looks back is fit for service in the Kingdom of God."**

Those of you who know something about plowing know that, in plowing, whether it is a plow that is pulled by a mule, work horses, or by a diesel tractor know that there is one thing you don't do in the process of plowing – you never try to plow while looking over your shoulders,. If you do, you then become unfocused on the task ahead and the rows that you plow become crooked and your field becomes difficult to work.

Farmers know that, if it is your habit of plowing while looking back, you're not fit to be in the field. And if you work for a farmer, working like that, you'd be fired by that farmer, for the object of plowing is to fix your eyes on a point at the far end of the field and then move steadily or progressively in that direction, not veering to the right side or swerving to the left side. And *"to put your hand to the plow"* means that you simply begin the work of plowing, or tilling the ground, or cultivating the field, and the Greek verb tenses, as it relates to plowing emphasize the point. **"No man, having put"** is an Aorist tense, or it is a past complete action, and the phrase, **"and looking back"** is a Present tense, or it denotes a continuous action; therefore, it is a continuous action that makes one unfit.

Here in our text, Jesus isn't saying that you cannot glance back, but He is saying that you cannot continue to look back once you've put your hand to the plow and begun the task of plowing, for if you do, you're not fit, or you become unsuitable for the task at hand. And like the task of plowing, following Jesus and becoming a member of the Church and citizen of the Kingdom is not a light matter, but rather something that must be taken seriously, even in our day, when we are inundated with a message of *"cheap grace,"* that is in conflict with what we hear from Scripture and from Jesus Himself.

"Cheap grace" is a promise of God's blessings without any consideration or calculation of personal cost. In his book entitled, *"The Cost of Discipleship,"* Dietrich Bonhoeffer, who was a German Lutheran pastor and author, declares:

"Cheap grace is the preaching of forgiveness without requiring repentance; it is baptism without church discipline; it is communion without confession; it is absolution without personal confession. Cheap grace is grace without

discipleship; it is grace without the Cross; it is grace without Jesus Christ; cheap grace is grace without having to give up anything or change anything."

And for years people have been lured into the church and manipulated into giving massive amounts of money by this message and promise of *"cheap grace"* – just *name it and claim it,* and you can *call it and haul it* – just say to yourself: *money cometh to me now* – just *sow your seed of faith and you can reap your harvest of material possessions,* without so much as sounding the alarm of Kingdom commitment, or life transformation, or God's demand for holiness, obedience, fidelity, humility, self-sacrifice, and involvement. This message is popular because it is in sync with the will of many, who desire benefit without commitment, or dividend without investment, or pleasure without problem, or riches without work. These are they, who buy the lotto tickets, and who frequent the riverboats, and who run down the aisles of our churches and throw money on the altar thinking that to be sufficient for the favor of God, and who look for easy remedies and undemanding religions to accommodate and appease their thirst for life and ministry ease, comfort, prosperity, and possession. Such people are looking for a comfortable and convenient Christianity, or for a Christianity that allows them the privilege of cameo appearance, sporadic giving, and a sermon that will feed itching ears, embrace sinful lifestyles and not address the injustices of the world. They look for a church, where they can go in without having to fit in, make contributions, personal commitment, sacrifice or obligation.

I've heard people say, *"I would do, but I don't want to commit myself, or I don't want to obligate myself – just let me be, let me think about it, let me pray on it for a little while,"* and they do this for the rest of their lives. Yet they show up but they won't serve. They show up but they won't give. They show up but sit back and spectate instead of participating, and having received, they never want to reciprocate. This is the way of *"cheap grace."* This is the way of having faith without works. This is the way of saying to Jesus, **"I will follow you wherever you go,"** yet when the time comes to go or when He beckons us to come, other things become priority.

Cheap grace is an enemy of the Church. *Cheap grace* is a detriment to the cause. *Cheap grace* is a hindrance to the authenticity of the Gospel, and its message is in opposition to the message of Christ. Hear the words of Jesus concerning our commitment to the Kingdom:

- *If anyone would come after Me, he must deny himself and take up his cross and follow Me* (Matt 16:24, Mark 8:34, Luke 9:23 – all NIV)
- *Seek first the Kingdom of God and all its righteousness* (Matt 6:33, NIV)
- *Anyone who loves his father or mother more than me is not worthy of Me, and anyone who loves his son or daughter more than Me is not worthy of Me* (Matt 10:37, NIV)

In contrast to *"cheap grace,"* the expectation of the Kingdom is *"costly grace."* *Costly grace* entails commitment. *Costly grace* requires obligation. *Costly grace* necessitates sacrifice and it demands the advantage of priority. *Costly grace* is what Jesus is looking for from those of us who follow Him; from those of us who acknowledge Him; from those of us who bear His Name and claim Him as Lord. Once we accept Him and have been baptized in His Name, then there comes responsibility with the privilege of Kingdom membership.

The cost of this grace, the grace that is God's grace, is the cost of dedication. It is the cost of one's life. It is the cost of self-denial and the cost of:

- Enlistment
- Service
- Comfort zone squeeze
- Giving Jesus the 'right of way' everyday and in every way

This grace is costly because it cost God His Only Son, and it cost Jesus His sinless life. And what cost God much and Jesus His life cannot be cheaper for you and I. The Word says, **"Hereby perceive we the love of God, because He laid down His life for us, we ought to lay down our lives for the cause"** (1 John 3:16, NIV). And when I ponder the text before us, I ponder the fact that, far too many are too busy to follow Christ. I ponder the fact that, we're too occupied with world endeavors. I ponder the fact that, we're too focused on material stuff, too attached to people and temporal things, too attached to fame and fortune and too possessed and obsessed with selfishness. When I consider the charge of Christ that we **"go, and make disciples"** (Matt 28:19) – that we **"love one another"** (John 13:35) – that we help our fellow man and be about our Father's business. There is no cost that is too great and nothing else more important.

- Kingdom commitment is a commitment to evangelize
- Kingdom commitment is a pledge to tell His story
- Kingdom commitment is a vow to forsake all others. It says: *for God I live and for God I die,* and it will **"press toward the mark of the high calling in Christ Jesus"** (Phil 3:14)
- It comes to know the Word of God
- It comes to worship the Name of God
- It comes to give in gratitude
- It comes grow in God's grace

When I think about Kingdom commitment, I think about Jesus Christ. The Bible says, **"That He made Himself nothing, took on the nature of a servant; that He humbled Himself in service, and became obedient unto death"** (Phil 2:7-8). I hear the Lord say, **"I must work the works of Him that sent Me, while it is day; the night cometh, when no man can work"** (John 9:4). It's that time. It's time to work. It's time to serve. It's time to give and time to commit. The Word says, **"Commit thy ways unto the LORD; trust in Him, and He will do this"** (Psalm 37:5, NIV). Do what? The LORD will give you the desires of your heart. The LORD will make the crooked straight. The LORD will turn your life around if only we commit to Him, His Way, His Word, and to His Kingdom.

"NOT EVERY ONE THAT SAITH UNTO ME, LORD, LORD, SHALL ENTER INTO THE KINGDOM OF HEAVEN; BUT HE THAT DOETH THE WILL OF MY FATHER WHICH IS IN HEAVEN."
(MATTHEW 7:21)

Jesus of Nazareth

Chapter 2: Sermon Two

Kingdom Greatness

(First Preached — True Foundation Transformation Church — 3/30/08)

Matthew 20:20-28

"Then the mother of Zebedee's sons came to Jesus with her sons and, kneeling down, asked a favor of Him. (21) "What is it you want?" He asked. She said, "Grant that one of these two sons of mine may sit at your right and the other at your left in your Kingdom." (22) "You don't know what you are asking," Jesus said to them. "Can you drink the cup I am going to drink?" "We can," they answered. (23) Jesus said to them, "You will indeed drink from My cup, but to sit at My right or left is not for Me to grant. These places belong to those for whom they have been prepared by My Father." (24) When the ten heard about this, they were indignant with the two brothers. (25) Jesus called them together and said, "You know that the rulers of the Gentiles lord it over them, and their high officials exercise authority over them. (26) Not so with you. Instead, whoever wants to become great among you must be your servant, (27) and whoever wants to be first must be your slave, (28) just as the Son of Man did not come to be served, but to serve, and to give His life as a ransom for many.""

The desire and pursuit of greatness has been an endearing and fixated craving of mankind since our creation. It was the appeal of becoming something more than what we are within the Garden of Eden that drew us to break the one commandment that God gave us: **"And the LORD God commanded the man, saying, Of every tree of the garden thou mayest freely eat: But of the tree of the knowledge of good and evil, thou shalt not eat of it: for in the day that thou eatest thereof thou shalt surely die"** (Gen 2:16-17, KJV). And in the aftermath of such pursuit, we then infected and injected the world with death, disease, and with natural disasters and division, which all stemmed from the temptation of self-elevation and an awakened inner yearning to be in the place of God, supreme, in power, autonomous and in essence, great. The psalmist says, **"Great is the LORD, and greatly to be praised; and His greatness is unsearchable"** (Psalm 145:3). It is no secret that, from the very outset to the very present, people have been infatuated with this greatness, prominence, notoriety, superiority, privilege, power and prestige. As a matter of fact, such obsession has been the cause of many wars, crimes, broken fellowships, friendships, families, and church splits.

There are people, who even leave the church because they have been smitten with a quest to gain more than what the church offers, or of what their gift provides, and of what the *Kingdom* promises. They once were a part of us and among us, but they are no more in our midst or with us because they wanted more of what the world enticed them with, in terms of fame and fortune; far more than what they gained or gleaned, according to them, from the church.

This search for greatness is all around us. It is the reason why so many of us are addicted and give much success and ratings to such present-day television programs as: American Idol, the Apprentice, America's Next Top Model, TMZ, Inside Edition, and the list go on. We want to be or are infatuated with celebrities and or with star status. We want people to notice us, or to swoon over us, and as some people desire managerial positions in the corporate world, some of these are those, who simply crave them to be in authority and have clout over people. Oh, they say it's about the money, but with some it's about the title and the power, which is also present within the church.

This is just me, but I believe a small percentage of people go into law enforcement, politics, and even into church ministry, not out of a sense of calling to serve and to protect, or to help and to edify, or to legislate and govern in favor of the people, but with an inner inkling and impulse of getting to a place "above the law" and *above the people,* or to a place of perks and license, reputation and societal status. Some people just want to be famous. Some people want to be looked upon with high regard. Some people want to be given special attention, notice, and consideration. Some want the nurse to get the juice and wipe the sweat, and the body guards to look important or the designation to deem significant. And then there are some, who may not seek the top spot or the central position, but yet they still lobby for the place or appointment of favor and deputy, control and influence, at either the right or left side of those in charge, with a preference for the right side over the left side, which is routinely the side reserved for the second-in-command. This is the type of attitude and aspiration that Jesus addresses within our text as He is approached with a request for these seats of distinction and entrustment.

The communication of this incident is recorded for us in two separate and somewhat parallel accounts within Scripture, here in Matthew Chapter 20, with the other in Mark Chapter 10. I chose the record of Matthew simply because its story line adds another character into the equation of request that is not mentioned in Mark's account.

In Matthew 20, verses 20 and 21 it states that: **"The mother of Zebedee's sons came to Jesus with her sons and, kneeling down, asked a favor of Him,"** saying: **"Grant that one of these two sons of mine may sit at your right and the other at your left in your Kingdom,"** and it should not surprise us to see a mother looking out for what she perceives to be the best interests of her children. Mothers tend to do that. They want the best for us. They desire better for their sons and daughters, and we cannot fault them for that, it's just a part of them and ingrained within them. It is a deep-seated and deep-rooted drive on the inside of perhaps all true mothers that pushes them into their children's business and propels them to become the spokesperson, either by permission or without permission, on their children's behalf. And so, it's not surprising to see a mother approaching Jesus on behalf of her sons, for mothers are like that. As a matter of fact, what better way of getting Jesus to agree with ones' appeal than to have your mother ask on your behalf, some even speculating that this mother of the disciples James and John was also Jesus' aunt, the sister of Mary, the mother of Jesus.

Can you hear her say, *"Excuse me, my dear nephew – can you do me a favor?"* But those of us, who know Jesus from the context of Scripture, know that if He can say to His mother, **"what have I to do with thee"** (John 2:4), when approached by Mary for favors for others, He then would have no problem saying *"not so"* to His aunt. And can you imagine the chaos, if Jesus would have said *"yes?"* It would have created another problem between these two brothers and the rest of Jesus' disciples.

A "yes" would have pitted James and John against each other for the first chair, the right seat, and it would have created more dissension than what already existed between the Twelve, as James and John would say to them, *"we be the man,"* and the other ten would then rise up against them for beating them to the punch, for James and John were not the only ones, who had their eyes on these seats.

Examine the response of the other disciples. They were outraged by the request made of James and John to Jesus. They were gnashing their teeth. They were upset. They were infuriated and enraged and somewhat ready to fight; not because they had a righteous indignation toward James and John, nor because they were so humble, meek and modest in and of themselves, but the other disciples were jealous, envious, resentful and aggrieved, all because John, James and their mother spoke up first and beat them to it.

Note that the Bible informs us, in **Mark 9:34**, in **Luke 9:46**, and again in **Luke 22:24** that all of Jesus' disciples disputed or argued among themselves, which of them would be or were considered by Jesus to be the greatest.   And in **Matthew 18:1**, not long before the events of our text, it is noted that they all came to Jesus inquiring of Him, **"Who is the greatest in the Kingdom of Heaven?"** No, the other disciples were by no means without self-ambition, self-interest, or self-desire. They too craved *Kingdom* greatness. They too yearned for power and for prestige. They too had aspirations of grandeur, and their eyes were also set on these seats of rank and authority. They were simply mad at the fact that James and John had the aggressiveness and audacity to state on the outside what they all had ambition for on the inside. And if the truth be told, such are some of us. Like all of the Twelve, we too have ambitions, and like all of the Twelve, we too have aspirations, and like all of the Twelve, we too crave sometimes for prominence and to be counted among those considered to be important, significant, noteworthy, and in authority. And with some of us, if we don't get the attention or demand we crave, like children we spout, and like children we cry, and like children we throw tantrums and our facial expressions display our irritations, frustrations, and disgust.

But listen church, I've discovered that, ambition, aspiration, dreams and desires can also be a good thing. In and of themselves, these are not the problem of our text, but the crisis lies in the motive and intent of the ambitions of James and John, and don't forget, the other ten. And

I believe the point that Jesus seeks to convey within our text, beyond giving us a clear and precise definition of *Kingdom* greatness and beyond reversing the role of the world's standards on such is that, I believe Jesus also communicates to us that, the right kind of ambition is that which brings glory to God and not to ourselves. It is that, which builds others up and not we. It is that, which invest itself in the welfare of others. It is that, which pours out itself into others. It is that, which uplifts. It is that, which enhances. It is that, which restores. It is that, which has as its aim not the personal benefit and promotion of self nor the applause and accolades of people, but that which strengthens the faith and lives of others to the glory of God and representation of Christ. It is an ambition that seeks to walk in the shoes of Jesus. It is an ambition, which exemplifies the mindset of Jesus. It is ambitions that performs the works of Jesus, and let's not forget, it is one which seeks to carry its own cross like Jesus. Hear Him say: **"If any man will come after Me, let him deny himself, take up his cross, and follow Me"** (Matt 16:24, KJV).

We must understand, *Kingdom* greatness does not come without cost, requirement, or duty. Jesus told James and John, **"You don't know what you request. Can you drink of the cup I am about to drink from?"** And besides this, although you will, it is not Mine to assign – **"to sit at My right or left is not for Me to grant,"** but **"these belong to those for whom the Father has prepared them for."**

Kingdom greatness is not something we get by simply asking the King of the Kingdom for it. *Kingdom greatness* is not something we get because of who we're related to. *Kingdom greatness* is not something we gain because of who may ask on our behalf. It is not about connection. It is not about precedence or preference. It is not about ability, money, power, position, or prestige, but it's reserved for those, who give themselves in service to others. It's about servanthood and sacrifice. It's about ministry and surrender. It's about self-denial and people-focus. It's about being like Jesus Christ. And Jesus said, **"Just as the Son of Man did not come to be served, but to serve"** (Matt 20:28), so you and I must do the same. It's not about who serves us, but it's all about who we serve. Kingdom greatness is about:

- Washing your neighbor's feet
- Patching your neighbor's wounds
- Healing your neighbor's heart
- Helping your fellowman

So you want to be great in God's Kingdom, then you must count the cost to be the boss. You cannot bypass the servant's quarters and sidestep our duty to others. I heard Jesus say, **"Inasmuch as you do it to the least of these, you do it unto Me"** (Matt 25:40). Do what? Feed the hungry. Do what? Clothe the naked. Do what? Shelter the homeless. Do what? Love ye one another.

Jesus came not for Himself, but He came for someone else. He came on our behalf, and He came for our good.

- He came to heal the brokenhearted
- He came to set the captives free
- He came to give sight to the blind, make the lame to walk and the mute to talk, and Jesus came to preach the Gospel
- He came to clothe the naked
- He came to feed the hungry
- He came to defend the defenseless, invite in the outcast, provoke justice, and to give His life for our sins
- He washed His disciples feet
- He gave comfort to the comfortless
- He lifted up the downtrodden, and He showed us how to serve
- He served, when He was lied on
- He served, when He was talked about
- He served, when was criticized
- He served, unto the Cross, and even on Calvary's cross, He yet served on our behalf: **"He was wounded for our transgressions; He was bruised for our iniquities; the chastisement of our peace was laid upon Him and through His stripes, we've been healed"** (Isaiah 53:5). It's all about service, ministry, helping someone out, someone up, and about helping someone through.

If you want to be great in the Kingdom of God; the songwriter says:

A charge to keep I have; a God to glorify; an ever-dying soul to save; to be fitted for the sky; to serve this present age, our calling to fulfill, and may it all our power engaged, to do our Master's Will.

*If I can help somebody as I pass along; if I can cheer somebody
with a word or song; if I can show somebody that they're
traveling wrong, then my living is not in vain.*

And when it's all said and done, I want to hear Jesus say, **"Servant,
well done."**

AFTER THIS MANNER THEREFORE PRAY YE: OUR FATHER WHICH ART IN HEAVEN, HALLOWED BE THY NAME. THY KINGDOM COME. THY WILL BE DONE IN EARTH, AS IT IS IN HEAVEN. (MATTHEW 6:9-10)

Jesus of Nazareth

CHAPTER 3: SERMON THREE

KINGDOM PRIORITIES

(FIRST PREACHED — TRUE FOUNDATION TRANSFORMATION CHURCH — 4/6/08)

MATTHEW 6:33

**"But seek ye first the Kingdom of God, and His righteousness;
and all these things shall be added unto you."**

One of the most popular memory verses in all of Scripture is the verse of our text, and rightly so because it speaks to the promise of God, as it has to do with making provisions for the preoccupations that we tend to have within life. Such preoccupations as noted in Scripture as: **1)** What we shall eat, and **2)** What we shall drink, and **3)** The concerns we have for the body; how we shall clothe ourselves or what we shall wear, now coupled with some others during this modern day economic recession and money deficiency.

Beyond the basic needs of food, drink, and clothing, people are on edge, nervous, and worried about mortgage payments, health insurance, tuition cost, gas prices, medical expenses, home foreclosures, job security, grocery bills, utility expenditures, and the list goes on. With already 225,000 jobs lost this year and with a reduction in the work force comes an increase in the statistics of crime, suicide, depression and anxiety. People seek other means of survival or simply worry about how they will survive. Even still, some others close the life book and give up hope on trying altogether. In many ways, the verse of our text is an inoculation or injection of optimism in the midst of doubtful situations, and it lifts up divine assurance as remedy for human uncertainties, worldly cares, individual questions and universal inquiries. Yet, we must also keep in mind that this promise of provision is not without stipulation. Remember David said: **"I once was young, but now I'm old, and I've never seen the righteous forsaken, nor his seed begging bread"** (Psalm 37:25). In other words, never lose sight of the fact that, Kingdom promise demands Kingdom living and that Kingdom living necessitates we have proper priorities. It all rises and falls right here. *Priority* is the difference between window blessings and token benefits, and where *priority* is misplaced or misappropriated; God's promise is not obligated.

Know that, there is a difference between living in the promises and benefiting from the premises. Some of us are merely surviving from the residuals of someone else. A "residual" is a leftover. A *residual* is something that's left behind. It's surplus. It's an oversupply. A *residual* is something extra, 'in addition to.' something that remains, lingers, a remnant, scraps, snippets and bits and pieces. *Residuals* are the crumbs that fall from someone else's plate.

Whereas it may be good to get an inheritance or a handout, you ought to want something of your own accord, from your own labors, that points to your faith, pinpoints your faithfulness, identifies your trust and conviction, and dependency upon God. You ought to want something God-given to you because it is your priorities that are in line with His will for your life. Not something from your mother. Not something because of your father. Not something from the faithfulness of those around you, but something 'to you' because of 'you.' The songwriter says: *"Momma may have, and papa may have, but God bless the child, who's got his own."* I'm talking about "Kingdom Priorities."

This often quoted verse of Scripture is a summary of the context of communication expounded upon by Jesus within this chapter, which begins at verse 19 and is somewhat brought to a close with verse 34. I say, 'somewhat brought to a close' simply because, the context here is part of a much larger framework of teaching that is ascribed to Jesus and known to us as *"The Sermon on the Mount,"* which encompasses the written contents of Chapters 5, 6, and 7 of Matthew's Gospel account of the ministry and message of Jesus.

In Chapter 5 the spotlight is on the blessings and responsibilities of Kingdom citizens, which then evolves at the beginning of Chapter 6 into a discussion and instructions on how to, **1)** properly perform acts of religious virtue, **2)** directives concerning prayer, and **3)** giving us information on fasting; all of which Jesus says, *should be done without fanfare, in secret before God, and as worship to God.* Then the theme shifts to "priorities" – *priorities* in the sense that the subject matter now centers on first concern and allegiance, and on ones' principal focus and pursuits within life.

- **"Do not store up for yourselves treasures on earth, where moth and rust destroy, and where thieves break in and steal. But store up for yourselves treasures in Heaven, where moth and rust do not destroy, and where thieves do not break in and steal. For where your treasure is, there your heart will be also"** (Matthew 6:19-21).

- **"No one can serve two masters. Either he will hate the one and love the other, or he will be devoted to the one and despise the other. You cannot serve both God and Money"** (Matthew 6:24).

- **"Therefore I tell you, do not worry about your life, what you will eat or drink; or about your body, what you will wear. Is not life more important than food, and the body more important than clothes"** (Matthew 6:25)?

- **"But seek ye first the Kingdom of God, and His righteousness; and all these things** (the things we worry about and pursue in life) **shall be added unto you"** (Matthew 6:33).

In all of this there is a subtle reminder that, we cannot accommodate 2 kingdoms in the same space of time, affection, and attachment. In other words, it cannot be the kingdoms of this world and the Kingdom of God, and worry, brought about by the preoccupations of life, cannot occupy the same mind and thought as confidence in God and dependence upon God. Jesus taught us to say: **"Our Father, Who art in Heaven, hallowed be Thy Name, Thy Kingdom come, Thy Will be done, on earth, as it is in Heaven"** (Matthew 6:9-10). After this to say: **"give us this day our daily bread"** (Matthew 6:11), taking no thought for the provisions of tomorrow but keeping our focus on today, as we keep our focus on the Kingdom.

Another subtle reminder is that, we cannot have a double standard of values, or worry about materialistic supplies, or fret over tomorrow's needs, nor chase gold before or in place of God. As a matter of fact, within the context of our text, Jesus asserts the priority of the Kingdom to be the Kingdom, and He instructs those of us, who assert membership in this Kingdom to make the Kingdom priority within our lives, along with the concerns of the Kingdom and what it is that identifies us with the Kingdom. And so we have no misunderstanding, know that, the most important characteristic of the Kingdom is "righteousness": **"But seek ye first the Kingdom of God and His righteousness."**

Righteousness is not just acts or what we do, but it is also disposition or who we are. It is not just when other people are around but even when we are all by ourselves – in the house alone with the blinds closed and the curtains drawn. We are to be righteous when we're on exotic cruises, thousands of miles from the church and from the people of the church. Righteousness entails a twofold quality of linkage and association – one with God and the other with mankind, and they are both intertwined and interrelated, the one to the other.

In other words, you cannot separate the two. *Righteousness* is about being right with God and being right with mankind. The Word says:

- **"How can you say you love God, whom you've never seen, and hate your brother, who you see everyday"** (1 John 4:20)?
- **"If you forgive men when they sin against you, your Heavenly Father will also forgive you. But if you do not forgive men their sins (against you), your Father will not forgive your sins (against Him)"** (Matthew 6:14-15).

God gave us 10 commandments – the first 4 deal with our relations with Him, while the last 6 point to our relations with those around us, who look like us, feel like us, hurt like us, and die like us.

Righteousness is a very important concept within the Kingdom of God, and it is a part of the grand scope of things within Heaven we should make priority here on earth, as we seek first God's Kingdom. And so we grasp the magnitude of such requirement, in Matthew 5:20 Jesus declares unto His disciples: **"Unless your righteousness surpasses that of the Pharisees and teachers of the Law, you will certainly not enter the Kingdom of Heaven."** And Chapter 6 begins with a warning against the deeds of our righteousness being done for the glory and attention of men. This was the way of the Pharisees and the teachers of the Law. They were hypocritical and deceitful, insincere and phony. They reduced the demands of God into a convenient and controllable list of rules and regulations, and they put burdens on the people that they did not bear themselves. In other words, they spoke one thing but they did another. They proclaimed, but they did not practice. They stated the requirements of God, but they exempted themselves from application. The Apostle Paul declares in Romans 10:2: **"they had a zeal of God, but not according to knowledge,"** and instead of submitting themselves unto the righteousness (or standards) of God, they established their own codes (or standards) of righteousness. Lesson for us: *'It's not righteousness unless it's done God's way.'*

In other words, there is no Burger King philosophy or privilege among the value systems of God. We cannot be a part of the Kingdom and then ignore or omit out of our lives, the total requirements of the Kingdom. In other words, we cannot substitute what **"Thus says the LORD"** with 'he say,' 'she say,' 'they say,' and what 'we say.' And we have no vote on the **"Thou shalt nots,"** and there are no loopholes in the requirements of God

Kingdom priority asserts that, we put God first and seek Him before all else. It claims our attention. It demands our focus. It insists that we **"have no other gods before Him"** (Exodus 20:3), and that we go after Him and make haste to please God.

Kingdom priority is about pursuing the Kingdom as 'priority.' It maintains exclusive right. It is firm on wholistic devotion. It is adamant, when it comes to allegiance. It wants the Tithe. It wants our time. It desires the best of us – the best of our talents, gifts, worship and praise. The psalmist says: **"I will praise Thee, O LORD, with my whole heart"** (Psalm 9:1). Jesus said: **"Love the LORD, with your whole heart, mind and strength"** (Matthew 22:37). This is what the Kingdom requires of us, that we **"seek first God's Kingdom."** If we seek it, we shall find it, and once we've found it, all else becomes secondary.

- God then becomes first
- His Will is number one
- His Word is number one
- His Son is number one
- Your service is at His service

- It is no longer 'my will,' but it's **"Thy will be done."**

- Your steps are ordered by the Lord
- Your life is hidden behind the Cross

- You adjust your prayer life
- You increase your fellowship
- You escalate your giving, and you augment your thankfulness.

If the Kingdom is priority, then the temporal becomes minor and the eternal becomes major. You sit self down and lift Jesus up. You move self back and bring Jesus forward. You shut self in and bring Jesus out. You declare His goodness. You proclaim His Gospel. You announce His purpose and exemplify who Jesus is

Jesus is the King of the Kingdom, and I salute my King. I give honor to my King. My King made me a priority with His life, and I will make my life a priority for Him. I challenge you to do the same.

AS YE GO, PREACH, SAYING, THE
KINGDOM OF HEAVEN IS AT HAND.
(MATTHEW 10:7)

Jesus of Nazareth

CHAPTER 4: SERMON FOUR

KINGDOM INVESTMENTS

(FIRST PREACHED — TRUE FOUNDATION TRANSFORMATION CHURCH — 4/13/08)

MATTHEW 6:19-20
(NIV)

"Do not store up for yourselves treasures on earth, where moth
and rust destroy, and where thieves break in and steal. (20) But
store up for yourselves treasures in Heaven, where moth and rust
do not destroy, and where thieves do not break in and steal."

*In Keeping with my Kingdom theme; thus far we've talked about
"Kingdom Commitment," "Kingdom Greatness," and "Kingdom
Priorities," and today we add a discussion on "Kingdom Investments."*

Many of us are familiar with the concept of "investment," and for those
among us who are not – investments are calculated to produce increase,
some great, some small, but nevertheless – increase. It is an enterprise with
an expectation of profit in which, an asset is purchased, stock is acquired,
or money is deposited into a bank or financial institution of such, all in
hopes of getting a future return of something more, or of something of
greater worth than its original pay in, down payment, or deposit.

As it relates to property or material possessions, you want to invest in
something that appreciates in value, goes up in price, or in something, if

evaluated over time, will make you richer than your present state. And in respect of currency, or mutual funds, or certificates of deposit, and other forms of financial endeavors, investments are made with an anticipation of receiving a yield, or a dividend check above and beyond ones investment.

The term "investment" itself infers that the safety of principal or that the protection of the initial investment is important to the investor. In other words, sound-minded people don't invest with the intention of losing. If they cannot gain, than the least that is expected is to break even. However, any investment counselor or firm will warn us that there is no investment without risk, and that any risk is not fail-safe. The more the investment, with an incentive expectancy of greater return, the greater the increase of the risk we take.

Key also to investments is, what we in invest in and where we invest, what it is we invest, and yet, placement of investment and exchange agent still does not negate risk or guarantee success. Possibility and chance are woven into the portfolio of any investment and as such, I don't believe that you can sue the stock market or the stock broker successfully if the stocks go down or if the market crashes – it's all a part of the risk that we take, when we make an investment. Sometimes we gain. Sometimes we lose. However, Jesus, within our text, brings us an exception to the rule. Here He highlights for us a Place, where all investments are secure, and a Place, where all things are eternal, and a Place, where there is no risk involved or possibility attached to what we invest, and where dividends are far greater than ever can be imagined here on earth.

In contrast to the insecurities of earthly wealth, properties, and possessions, and in contrast to the potential of decay, deterioration, and the consumption of all we treasure and hold dear within this world, Jesus points us upward and propositions us to rethink our course of actions, reorganize our life priorities, convert the treasures of earth into treasures within Heaven, thus obtaining for ourselves what only Heaven can guarantee us – true security and definitive return, without risk of all we invest and deposit into the treasuries of the Kingdom. And so we understand, what Jesus does not do within our text is that, He does not prohibit us or forbid and disallow us from providing for the necessities of life or from gaining wealth within life, nor does Jesus speak out within our text in opposition to us having things or desiring more than what we have at present. The problem is not with what we have or even with how much we have, but Jesus wants us to consider our use of what we have, and He also cautions us about putting our trust, and devoting our time, and expending our energies in areas and on things that are destined to end, dissolve, tarnish, or perhaps vanish into the hands of others, who set their eyes on the things we labor for, and who set their eyes on the things we make purchase of, and who set their eyes on the things we attempt to secure, at all cost, from them. These are they, who go to work when we leave for work, and these are they, who make it their profession to pillage from us the very things that we store up for ourselves within our homes. They are thieves and the robbers, burglars and crooks. They study us and survey our premises for opportune moments to break in and take out. In some cases, it's an inside job. In some cases it is people we trust and open our doors to, are related to, have given birth to, have friendship with, who know our children, live on the same block as us, worship with us and people who do service for us. Sometimes it's the people who break in and sometimes it's the people who are invited in.

How many know that it's one thing to take possession of something but another to protect that, which you have ownership of from thievery, corrosion, or from destruction that can be caused by the infestation of insects. Insects like "moths," which are butterfly-like creatures that sometimes feast on our clothes, or corrosion and destruction from old age, or from the normal wear and tear use of things that were never manufactured to last forever. As a matter of fact, all things attached to this world, though man may sell us lifetime guarantees at purchase, all such things can never be guaranteed by man for life. There was no safe and secure way at the time of our text and there is no sure safe and secure way now to warranty that no loss, damage, or decomposition befalls any and all that we own, take possession of, invest in, hide away, or lock up even now. As a matter of fact, that's why we buy insurance – life, health, home and automobile insurance. If the truth be told, lifetime guarantees are nothing but insurance policies so that, when what we buy breaks down and gives out, it can be replaced with minimum cost to us. Here again, all because nothing is guaranteed to last, stay in fit condition, or remain in our possession. The only assurance that we can have in life is that nothing in this world is assured.

- You can invest all of your time on a job, and that job can still cut you loose
- You can put all of your energy into a relationship, and that relationship can still be divorced – that man can still leave you and that woman can still walk away

- You can devote all of your attention to raising your children, giving them the best of everything and introducing them to the best of all things, and those children can still grow up and break your heart

Again, the only declaration of promise, from this world, in this world, and guarantee by this world is that, all that we have is only temporary. In other words, if it or they do not decay, we will, and what is not stolen from us will one day still be in the possession of someone else. Someone else will still drive our cars. Someone else will still wear our clothes. Someone else will still spend our money, and someone else will still sleep in our beds. We will die and we cannot take the things or people that we've grown attached to or fond of with us. Know that, generally gravesites are made for one – for one body, one set of clothes, one pair of shoes, one watch, one ring, one tie, one shirt, one dress, one suit and or one wig. 'You can only take one.' And it too, if it makes it in the ground, will also perish in the earth. So what do we do? So what should we do? Jesus says: **"Do not store up for yourselves treasures on earth," "but store up for yourselves treasures in Heaven."**

In other words, Jesus instructs us to make "Kingdom Investments," and a *Kingdom investment* is made, when we make investments on earth on behalf of the Kingdom. These are investments that bring glory to the Kingdom. These are investments, which lift up the standards of the Kingdom. These are investments that are representative or reflective of the King of the Kingdom.

- A *Kingdom investment* is made, when we use earthly money and time to help those in need
- A *Kingdom investment* is rendered, when we take the time to take groceries to a starving family
- A *Kingdom investment* comes about, as we go about: *nursing the sick, fellowshipping with the elderly, bringing Word to the lost and providing clothes to the naked*

- It's when we love our fellow man
- It's when we seek to forgive one another
- It's when we sacrifice on behalf of each other
- It's when we lift up the Name of Jesus

A *Kingdom investment* happens when:

- We give to charity
- We support the efforts of the local church
- We stand up for the defenseless, and when we speak up for the voiceless

- It's when we empty ourselves by pouring out into others
- It's when we sustain a missionary through financial support and prayer
- It's when we go beyond ourselves and extend ourselves, and when we shift the focus from the earthly to the heavenly and from the temporal to the eternal.

- A *Kingdom investment* happens when we serve this present age
- When we do our Christian duty
- When we answer the Christian call to **"make disciples of all nations"** (Matthew 28:20) and **"to go out into the highways and hedges and compel men to come in"** (Luke 14:23).

We make deposit in the vaults of Heaven, when "each one reaches out to one" – when we sow a Gospel seed for the salvation of a soul – when we encourage one another – when we build up each other. It happens when we tell the Gospel story of our Savior Jesus Christ. It's when we give out a Gospel tract. It's when we bring others to the church. It's when we lift up the blood-stained banner of the Cross. Make an investment today.

THE KINGDOM OF HEAVEN IS LIKENED UNTO A MAN WHICH SOWED GOOD SEED IN HIS FIELD.
(MATTHEW 13:24)

Jesus of Nazareth

CHAPTER 5: SERMON FIVE

KINGDOM FOCUS

(FIRST PREACHED – TRUE FOUNDATION TRANSFORMATION CHURCH – 4/20/08)

COLOSSIANS 3:1-2

(KJV)

"If ye then be risen with Christ, seek those things which are above, where Christ sitteth on the right hand of God. (2) Set your affection on things above, not on things on the earth."

(NIV)

"Since, then, you have been raised with Christ, set your hearts on things above, where Christ is seated at the right hand of God. (2) Set your minds on things above, not on earthly things."

The term "focus" gives reference to *"a point of convergence,"* a place of coming together. It speaks to that area or matter of fixation, which tends to garner our attention, or apprehend our concentration, or to that, which has the propensity to pull the faculties of our hearts, and of our minds, and of our eyes, our ears, and of our energies together into the same direction of attraction and of activity, and into the same dimension of thought, emotion, gaze and consideration. Its synonyms are: *meeting point, gathering place, hub, center, focal point and spotlight.* And when it is said that one is focused, the implication is made in such a statement that one is also attentive, or that one is also dutiful, or that one is also given to whatever the object or entity is of ones focus. And we all know that it is hard to focus on whatever it is we are attempting to focus on when we are distracted, diverted, or when we are divided in our allegiance of focus. This is especially true when it comes to spiritual things or Kingdom matters, such as: working on a sermon, reading ones Bible, finding a quiet moment of prayer and meditation to spend some time with God; coming to Bible study, being attentive when the preaching is going on during the Worship service, reviewing your Sunday school lesson, visiting the sick or being a witness to Christ, etc, etc, etc. There is something or someone always seeking to interrupt or divert our intent and focus away God and the task at hand, and to place them on things that are in opposition to God and in conflict with the things of God, or on things that have nothing to do with God. And the world and our days are filled with things and circumstances that are aimed at the Christian's focus. And the Apostle Paul, within our text, addresses the need for the reborn of Christ to redirect our interests and passions from earthly stuff to heavenly matters or from the temporal to the eternal, or from what's below to what's above, and from the carnal to the spiritual.

As a matter of fact, what's at issue within our text are the subjects of spirituality, relationship, position, union and priority, as Paul endeavors to convey, not only to the believers to whom he writes at Colossae (Ko-*loss*-ee), but also to all believers throughout all generations, who have been, as he talks about in Chapter 2, buried with Christ in baptism and then raised with Christ through the power of our faith in God, that having been thus raised with Christ: **1)** we have now become citizens of another world and **2)** such citizenship requires that we reprioritize our focus, adjust our behaviors, reorder our lives and that we follow the purpose of spiritual resurrection. *Spiritual resurrection* is the death of old things, thoughts, cravings and attractions, and the inauguration of that, which is new, in terms of attitudes, functions, desires and focus.   .

Spiritual resurrection, as symbolized through 'water baptism' and the 'baptism of the Holy Spirit' marks a rebirth or a beginning of a new life for the Christian, who now finds him or herself no longer in alliance with this world, but now in partnership with God's Kingdom. And as such, Paul stresses in Chapter 3 that, our walk or development, while yet still in this world, as Christians, should no longer be in accordance with this world but in alignment with and reflection of our newfound position and residency above. Better still, Paul goes on to say that, our affections, or our loves and fondnesses within this world should not be attached to this world or placed on this world, but rather on the things, which are of main concern and of decree within the Kingdom of God, such as: wholeheartedly being devoted to God, and giving exclusive worship to God, and loving ones neighbor as oneself, and being embodiments of all nine Fruit of the Spirit – *love, joy, peace, patience, kindness, goodness, faithfulness, gentleness, and self-control,* adding to these the spirit of a forgiving heart, and the gestures of a gracious and merciful mind, and the duty of an ambassador of the Kingdom, and the function of a true servant of the Gospel.

As Paul deals with the realms of Heaven and of earth, Paul deals with preeminence and loyalty, giving preference to the will and place of the Kingdom in the life of the Christian above the will and place of this world, not saying that heavenly things matter and earthly things don't, but rather challenging us, who have linked ourselves to Heaven through our acceptance of Jesus to make Christ and the Kingdom the center of our existence for the remainder of our stay here on earth on our pilgrimage to Heaven.

Scripture is clear. As a people of God, we are but *"pilgrims and strangers"* here on earth – sojourners in a foreign land – in the world but not of the world, and that we're looking for a city with foundations, whose builder and maker is God. It is all summed up in song, in that, *"this world is not our home."* This world is just a temporary residency as we simply pass through to glory land.

And so Paul says, **"seek those things which are above, where Christ sitteth on the right hand of God. Set your affection on things above, and not on earthly things."** And I think I told you on last Sunday that, everything attached to this world is only temporary. In other words, it will not last and that grave rules specify that, we can only take denominations of ones with us into the grave. We also stated that, all that makes it in the ground will perish in the earth because it came from the earth and belongs to the earth. Thus today we say, we cannot take what comes from the earth and what belongs to the earth beyond the earth. All earthly things must remain earthly and earthly-bound, and what does remain of the earth will all one day disappear. John said: **"I saw a new heaven and a new earth, for the first heaven and earth were passed away"** (Revelation 21:1). And so, rather than giving our attention to that, which will one day perish, the admonition is to **"seek those things which are above."** And the term *'seek'* is an action word, derived from the Greek phrase *"zeteo,"* which in connection with our text means to *"covet earnestly"* or to *"strive* *after,"* or to *"endeavor,"* and *"to desire"* greatly. And it signifies to us that, nothing is ever sought after or found unless some energy is burned and effort expended in its pursuit.

It's like the shepherd, who leaves the 99 sheep in search of the lost one, or the woman, who has 10 silver coins and loses one, but lights a candle and sweeps her house diligently until she recovers that, which was lost (note Luke 15). Paul, in like manner confronts us to *strive after and to covet earnestly the things which are above*, desiring and endeavoring to obtain and to place our focus on that, which is not from this earth, or on that, which belongs to this earth, nor on that, which can be restricted by the perimeters of this earth or dictated to by the residents of this earth. The admonition is to, look upward, and to make upward things pivotal or fundamental in our lives. In so doing, to engage ourselves in heavenly interests, goals and objectives, and to elevate our passions beyond the mere pursuit of the earthly and temporal, or beyond the mere pursuit of that, which will expire one day, or corrode one day, or simply vanish away with time? **"As the flowers fade and the grass withers"** (Isaiah 40:8), we too are but a vapor, which appears but for a season (note James 4:14).

The admonition within our text is to make Kingdom investments, and to have Kingdom commitment, and to aspire for Kingdom greatness, establishing Kingdom priorities, and to live life, here on earth, beyond the redemption of the Cross and the regeneration of baptism, on Kingdom terms. Without such an upward concentration, there can be no passionate motivation to **"seek first God's Kingdom and His righteousness"** (Matthew 6:33), or to honor the Kingdom agenda, or to pay respect to the Kingdom establishment, or to the Kingdom hierarchy or chain of command, and or to the Kingdom's King. This is why some Christians seek the earthly above the heavenly, because their mindset has not transcended the cravings of the flesh or exceeded the temptations of this world. To the carnal minded, gold comes before God and the persuasions of this world before the promises of God's Word.

Know that, everything related to our pursuits is interrelated with our focus. In other words, we tend to follow the will of the mind, that's why Paul says **"set your minds on things above,"** for thoughts give way to actions, and our actions are determined by our thoughts. The Bible says, **"For as he thinketh in his heart, so is he"** (Proverbs 23:7).

As Christians, it is our duties to position our minds and the affections of our hearts on heavenly things, for new life dictates that we inherit a new perspective, and that we take on new ambitions, and that we employ a new impulse, and occupy a new focus. 2nd Corinthians 5:17 declare: **"Therefore if any man be in Christ, he is a new creature: old things are passed away; behold all things are become new."**

Thus, as we've risen from the waters of baptism into the congregation of the saints:

- We must **"seek those things, which are above"**
- We must say: **"Our Father, Who art in Heaven, Hallowed be Thy Name, Thy Kingdom come, Thy will be done, in earth, as it is in Heaven"** (Matthew 6)
- We must take on the very mindset of Jesus Christ.
- We must strive to do God's will.
- We must fight for the faith
- We must promote the Kingdom program
- We must lift up another flag, that has the image of the Cross

As resurrected, new born believers, with a Kingdom focus and an upward deliberation, our aim must become new and our outlook should too. It is no longer about us but it becomes about Him. Our words become His words. Our thoughts become His thoughts. Our deeds become His deeds and our goals become His goals. We seek to go at God's command. We seek to move as He motivates and we seek to shift with His wind and transform as needed.

VERILY I SAY UNTO YOU, EXCEPT YE BE
CONVERTED, AND BECOME AS LITTLE
CHILDREN, YE SHALL NOT ENTER
INTO THE KINGDOM OF HEAVEN.
(MATTHEW 18:3)

Jesus of Nazareth

Chapter 6: Sermon Six

Kingdom Economics

(First Preached - True Foundation Transformation Church — 4/27/08)

Luke 6:38
(KJV)

"Give, and it shall be given unto you; good measure, pressed
down, and shaken together, and running over, shall men
give into your bosom. For with the same measure that
ye mete withal it shall be measured to you again."

(NIV)

"Give and it will be given to you. A good measure, pressed down,
shaken together and running over, will be poured into your lap.
For with the measure you use, it will be measured to you."

Many of us are aware that the economic situation here in the United States
is at an all time low. People from all walks of life are struggling to make
ends meet. People are struggling to provide for their families. People are
struggling to hold on to their homes. People are struggling with tuition
cost. People are struggling with medical expenses. People are struggling
with the basic necessities of daily living, and struggling with the high rate
of gasoline prices. I told you a few weeks ago in my message on *"Kingdom
Priorities"* that, people are nervous, and that people are on edge, and that

people are worried about survival, about expenditures, about their financial future, let alone their economic present. A squeeze is on, and not many of us are exempt from feeling the pinch of what is going on within each state of our nation as this subject matter of fiscal hardship is at the forefront of every debate within politics and the focal point of much discussion, and perhaps, divorce within our homes.

Since the inauguration of George W. Bush as the 43rd President of these United States in January of 2001, the cry of *"broke, busted, and disgusted"* has escalated, and its exclamation can be heard from the lips of African Americans, and from white America, and from the Hispanic community, the Asian community, and any other ethnic group within our country.

I think we all would agree that, at present, there is no shortage of lack, and we all would agree that the major complaint of today is that money is tight. Um hum, look at your neighbor and say: *'he's right, it's tight.'* And generally, when money is tight, people become *"tightwads."* *Tightwad* means, *"Cheap." Tightwad* means, *"Miserly." Tightwad* means *"tightfisted"* and *"stingy."* It describes a person who hoards what they have and is ungenerous about sharing. And I must say that, with some of us, even when we do have to the extent where giving of what we have will not hurt us or damage our economic stability, we are still *"cheap," "miserly," "tightfisted"* and *"stingy"* – hoarders of what we have and ungenerous about sharing, even when it comes to giving to the Lord, helping out family members, extending ourselves beyond ourselves and simply being a blessing to those that are truly in need. And in this, both in our deficient seasons and in our seasons of plenty, when we fail to operate according to the premise of the Kingdom, we then disqualify ourselves from the promise of our text, which states that, when we **"give,"** it shall be given unto us, in **"good measure, pressed down, shaken together, and running over"** return, which is simply a phrase that pronounces overabundance, not necessarily from those we give to, and yet sometimes it does happen. Sometimes those we give to gives back to us, again, sometimes. But if not from those who give to us it comes back as promised in abundance of our giving, for this is a divine principle that is resounded throughout all of Scripture - walk with me through the Word:

- Proverbs 3:9-10 proclaims: **"Honour the LORD with thy substance, and with the firstfruits of all thine increase: so shall thy barns be filled with plenty, and thy presses shall burst out with new wine."**

- Proverbs 11:25 declares: **"The liberal soul shall be made fat: and he that watereth shall be watered also himself."**
- Proverbs 22:9 affirms: **"A generous man will himself be blessed, for he shares his food with the poor."**
- Ecclesiastes 11:1 states: **"Cast thy bread upon the waters: for thou shalt find it after many days."**
- Isaiah 58:10 confirms: **"And if you spend yourselves in behalf of the hungry and satisfy the needs of the oppressed, then your light will rise in the darkness, and your night will become like the noonday."**
- Again, Luke 6:38 says: **"Give and it will be given to you. A good measure, pressed down, shaken together and running over, will be poured into your lap. For with the measure you use, it will be measured to you."**
- And then in 2nd Corinthians 9:6, as it relates to the measure of our giving it is written: **"Remember this: Whoever sows sparingly will also reap sparingly, and whoever sows generously will also reap generously."** In other words, our quantity of giving determines our ratio of return.

Kingdom economics sponsors this law within the Kingdom that, we get, when we give, and that, we get back in proportion to our giving. In other words, there are no dividends without provisions and you cannot expect a divine overflow, when you give in moderation or, when you decline to give at all. As a matter of fact, one of the rules of *Kingdom economics* demands that we relinquish limited resources to satisfy unlimited wants, as when a lad surrendered his lunch of **"two fish and five barley loaves"** (John 6:9) and Jesus then took the limited of the lad, blessed it to the glory of God, and in return fed multitudes of thousands, with 12 baskets of leftovers remaining (John 6:13).

Kingdom economics also has this rule that, the Kingdom prescribes the giving and that our giving must be in accordance with God's Word. Malachi 3:10 (NIV) says: **"Bring the whole tithe into the storehouse, that there may be food in My House. Test Me in this,"** says the LORD Almighty, **"and see if I will not throw open the floodgates of Heaven and pour out so much blessing that you will not have room enough for it."**

One critical lesson we must learn is that, giving is an act of worship that is naturally done outside of the species of man. The sun naturally gives us light, flowers naturally give us fragrance, bees give us honey, cows give us milk, chickens give us eggs, the waters give us fish, fruit trees yield their fruit, and even sheep are led to the slaughter without a fight.

Another lesson we must know is that, the ultimate recipient of our giving is God Himself. Is it not recorded in the Word, Proverbs 19:17: **"He who is kind to the poor lends to the LORD, and He (God) will reward him for what he has done"**? Did not Jesus say in Matthew 25: **"Verily I say unto you, Inasmuch as ye have done it unto one of the least of these My brethren, ye have done it unto Me."** Never dismiss the Heavenly connection of our earthly giving and in no way overlook the importance of giving. Jesus is quoted as saying in Acts 20:35: **"It is more blessed to give than to receive."** And God gives to us that we may in turn put into circulation, what He gives us, be it time or be it resources – the buck must not stop at us. As a matter of fact, circulation is the way of God. Things are designed to keep moving. Things are designed to keep progressing. Things are designed to keep growing and to keep changing. The Bible says: **"What has been will be again, what has been done will be done again; there is nothing new under the sun"** (Ecclesiastes 1:9, NIV). It all circulates and revolves.

'Giving' is the channel by which we collect and it is through release that we acquire increase, especially as it has to do with being a people of God, Kingdom citizens, subjects of another world and followers of Jesus Christ. Remember I stated on last week that, for those of us, who have been buried with Christ in baptism and raised with Him through the power of our faith in God, we have become citizens of another Kingdom, and as such, as citizens of God's Kingdom, we must operate in agreement with the regulations of His Kingdom, and the main regulation is that, we operate in faith, that we take God at His Word, that we trust and believe Him, and that, we deny ourselves for the sake of others. And recognize that, when we operate within the parameters of Kingdom specifications, then earthly conditions has no influence upon us. Let me see if I can put it in terms for understanding.

Regardless of what the economy is like within the realm of this world, and in spite of the fact that prices and payments are constantly rising, when we function as God determines, and when we execute as the Kingdom stipulates, no crisis on earth can overwhelm us that are His and no shortage of substance can preclude our survival. In testimony to this I hear David say: **"I have been young, and now am old; yet have I not seen the righteous forsaken, nor his seed begging bread"** (Psalm 37:25). One true fact of Kingdom economics is that, earthly economics are subject to God. **"The earth is the LORD's, and the fulness thereof; the world, and they that dwell therein"** (Psalm 24:1). In other words, God owns everything and He is always in control of all things. It may not look very bright, but for the advocate of God, everything will be alright. Um hum; testimony time.

- In the days of Joseph, though there was famine in Canaan, there was yet grain in Egypt (Genesis 42:1-), and though Elijah's brook dried up from lack of rain upon the land, there was a widow woman to sustain him, and because she sustained him, God sustained her (1 Kings 17:7-16). Lesson here: When you give much – you get much. When you give little – you get little. When you give nothing – you get nothing. Lesson here: Even when you don't have much and yet you still give, supply the needs of others, share what you have as a blessing to someone else, operate in faith and trust the Word of God for the provisions of God, then your little becomes much and your *jug* and *jar* will always be supplied.

Know that, even during the times of bad economy, it pays to be a giver because, when you give, God then becomes your provider and His Warehouse your warehouse. When you give, God will nourish you, and God will assist you, and God will shelter you, and He will make sure that, **"no weapon that is formed against thee shall prosper"** (Isaiah 54:17). Though others may suffer lack, Paul says: **"But my God shall supply all your need according to His riches in glory by Christ Jesus"** (Philippians 4:19). In other words:

- In unemployment, He'll meet your bills
- In hard times, He'll see you through
- In complicated situations, He'll resolve your difficulties, and in rough waters, God will calm your seas, rebuke the wind, and say: **"Peace, be still."**

As a child of God our problems reside not with worldly situations, but in whether or not we are obedient to God's standards of economy.

Some people prosper because they give and some people worsen because they do not. **"Be not deceived, God is not mocked, for whatsoever a man soweth, that shall he also reap"** (Galatians 6:7).

The kingdom of America and the Kingdom of God are two different realms, and what comes from Washington cannot compare to what gushes from Heaven. People are excited about stimulus checks; however, **"eye have not seen, nor ear heard, the good things, which God has laid up for them who love Him"** (1 Corinthians 2:9). I hear Jesus say: **"I am come that they might have life and that more abundantly"** (John 10:10). Paul says: **"Now unto Him that is able to do exceeding abundantly, above all that we can ask or think"** (Ephesians 3:20). But you must first sow a seed in order to gather a harvest – no seed, no harvest – no planting, no reaping. But if you **"give, it shall be given, in good measure, pressed down, shaken together and running over."** As we operate within the system of God's Kingdom.

- What we expect, we must give
- When in need, we must give
- To God's delight, we must give
- In all things and with all things, we must give

- We must give of our substance
- We must give of our services
- We must give of our time, and give of our gifts, and give of our talents, and give of our treasures. And when we give we gain a windfall, which flows back into our lap. It's a boomerang effect, what we send out comes back: *return to sender with interest.*

- It comes back with surplus
- It comes back with added bonus
- It comes back with increase
- It comes back with much more. So give out that you might get. Give some clothes away. Give some shoes away. Feed the hungry. Be a friend. Share the Gospel. Be a blessing to someone else, and the God of all riches shall deliver your needs, **"according to His riches in glory."** And how rich is our God?

- "The cattle on a thousand hills belong to Him" (Psalm 50:10)
- "The sea is His and He made it, and His hands formed the dry land" (Psalm 95:5)
- The LORD says: "The silver is Mine, and the gold is Mine" (Haggai 2:8)

How rich is our God? There's no lack in Heaven and no shortage of provisions. It pays to be a giver. It pays to help somebody. It pays to show love. It pays to do well. The Word says: **"Be not weary in well doing, for in due season, ye shall reap, if you faint not"** (Galatians 6:9). Therefore, keep on. Keep on putting out. Keep on sharing and caring. Keep on living and giving, and the Lord says, **"It will be given to you. A good measure, pressed down, shaken together and running over, will be poured into your lap. For with the measure you use, it will be measured to you"** (Luke 6:38).

SUFFER LITTLE CHILDREN, AND
FORBID THEM NOT, TO COME
UNTO ME: FOR OF SUCH IS
THE KINGDOM OF HEAVEN.
(MATTHEW 19:14)

Jesus of Nazareth

CHAPTER 7: SERMON SEVEN

KINGDOM PURPOSE

(FIRST PREACHED - TRUE FOUNDATION TRANSFORMATION CHURCH — 5/4/08)

JEREMIAH 1:1-5
(KJV)

"The words of Jeremiah the son of Hilkiah, of the priests that were in Anathoth in the land of Benjamin: (2) To whom the Word of the LORD came in the days of Josiah the son of Amon king of Judah, in the thirteenth year of his reign. (3) It came also in the days of Jehoiakim the son of Josiah king of Judah, unto the end of the eleventh year of Zedekiah the son of Josiah king of Judah, unto the carrying away of Jerusalem captive in the fifth month. (4) Then the Word of the LORD came unto me, saying, (5) before I formed thee in the belly I knew thee; and before thou camest forth out of the womb I sanctified thee, and I ordained thee a prophet unto the nations."

I think we all would agree that, many people, if not most people, go through life without any real sense of purpose, or without any real sense of knowing the rationale of their existence, or without coming into contact with some meaningful reason of their birth, or with some meaningful reason of their creative uniqueness, or with some meaningful reason why we dwell in the space and place of time between our birth and our death. Some people go their entire lives searching and experimenting, and dibbling and dabbling in all sorts of things and areas within life in an attempt to find their niche, or to find their place, or to discover their purpose in this universe.

We all know people, some that we work with, and some that we are friends with, and some, who are members of our families, who live life aimlessly, without any concrete goals, stated life agenda, positive ambitions, affirmative objectives, certain or definitive plans, or eschatological perspective. And don't get nervous, I'll define "eschatological."

"Eschatology" is a theological term which presents discourse or conversation about the last things. It is a study of the end of times, which deals with life after death issues and the end of the world. Within Christianity it covers such subjects as: the return of Christ, the gathering of the saints, the destruction of this world, the Day of Judgment, Eternal life or eternal damnation, and the final destination of Heaven or Hell. It is a school of thought, which teaches that all life and things move toward an end, and that there is something more to now, and that beyond now is a hereafter, which is based upon our existence in the now. *Eschatology* builds on the premise that life has purpose and responsibility, and with responsibility that, such life has accountability – and in Christianity, that all life must one day answer to God.

Into this, let me interject that, I believe, as it pertains to each of us that, it's no accident that we're here. I believe that no life has origin without God, regardless of how the life is orchestrated or no matter the method or intent of conception. God is still the initiator of all that is essential for a heart to beat, and for thoughts to take formulation, and for a soul to unite with a spirit and a body, and for us to come forth in life, with life.

In his book entitled "The Purpose Driven Life," author Rick Warren asserts this statement: *"Your birth was no mistake or mishap, and your life is no fluke of nature. Your parents may not have planned you, but God did. He was not at all surprised by your birth. In fact, He expected it. Long before you were conceived by your parents, you were conceived in the mind of God. He thought of you first. It was not fate, nor chance, nor luck, nor coincidence that you are breathing at this very moment. You are alive because God wanted to create you"* (p. 22). In other words, we are alive because God wanted us here. We are alive because God gave allowance for seed to be implanted within the womb of our mother. God may not have directed it because sometimes seed is implanted in sin, but nevertheless, God still gave exemption for it.

As it is declared by God in our text to the prophet Jeremiah, **"Before I formed thee in the belly I knew thee; and before thou camest forth**

out of the womb I sanctified thee," I believe also to be so with us, maybe not for the same purpose as Jeremiah, but before we were formed in the womb God knew us, and before we were born God set us apart. He sanctified us. God called us forth from the abyss of nothing to come forth out of the darkness of the womb and into the light of this world, I believe for – divine purpose. And yet, though many of us may not follow His purpose or fall in line with God's will for our birth, I still believe that there is *Kingdom purpose* for all life here on earth. I still believe that, all life originates in God, and that, all life proceeds from God, and that, all life has purpose in God, and that we are here for something more than merely the accumulation of things or the pursuit and build up of riches. I believe we are here for something more than the indulgences of worldly pleasures or even for the will of self. These all are only temporary gratifications that cannot fulfill or truly satisfy our real reason for being here.

God blew into our nostrils the breath of life for something greater and far meaningful than cars, clothes, the consumption of food and beverages, the attainment of houses and land, the quest for fame and distinction, the inheritance of titles and surnames, or for the explicit intent of obliging every and all craving of the flesh. As a matter of fact, if the truth be told, we tend to become bored and discontented with all such things after while. Let me see if I can come down your block.

- A new car is only new so long and then we want a new one. Clothes become unfashionable for many of us and then we want replacements. One meal does not satisfy the hunger of a whole day, and one drink does not quench the thirst of our need for liquids throughout an entire week.

Not in your neighborhood yet, let me continue:

- Our first house becomes our *first* house. Our first car becomes our *first* car. The mall becomes a hobby, and even with some of us, after a while sex is no big thing.

If the truth be told, we become bored with current things and we desire new things. We desire something bigger. We desire something better. We desire something faster, and something younger and more exciting. Why, because all temporal things is temporary. We were created eternal beings with an eternal purpose, and the temporal can never satisfy the eternal nor can the eternal be contented with the temporal.

Why do you think some billionaires and millionaires become unhappy with their riches and feel a need to share what they have with others? Rick Warren even said, though gaining millions from his books that it is his quest to leave this world broke. Why? Money is temporal and mankind is eternal and there is no lasting satisfaction with all that is attached to this world. Jesus said: **"What does it profit a man to gain the whole world and lose his soul"** (Matthew 16:26). There's something more to life than what this world has to offer. Um hum, I don't mean to burst your bubble however, there is something more than fur coats. There is something more than quick cash. There is something more than exotic beaches, and there is something more than diamond rings.

Know that life is not about us and stuff, but we were created by God for God. We were created for His purpose. We were created for His delight. We were created for His desire and for God's work, and until we come into *Kingdom purpose* or, until we allow our steps to be ordered by the LORD, I suggest that life can have no lasting fulfillment, permanent enjoyment, long-term contention or enduring accomplishment.

Yes, there will be moments of perks and peaks, but without God and without a central purpose in God, perks and peaks become burdens and valleys, a rollercoaster ride of highs and lows, of going up and of coming down, and of fabricated, manufactured thrills that are only for a moment – a moment of what you feel, when you do drugs – a moment of wooziness, when you get drunk – a moment of pleasure, after a night of promiscuity, and a moment of ecstasy after a moment of sin, debauchery, extravagance and over-spending. As a matter of fact, it is after such moments that many of us cry *"broke, busted, and disgusted."* We don't have any money left. We're bogged down with guilt. The bill collectors are hounding us, and some of us are sick now, diseased now, crippled now and unhealthy because of these moments of indulgences and thrill rides. You may not admit it but it's true. I'm included and so are you.

To quote Rick Warren again: *"It's not about you. The purpose of your life is far greater than your own personal fulfillment, your peace of mind, or even your happiness. It's far greater than your family, your career, or even your wildest dreams and ambitions. If you want to know why you were placed on this planet, you must begin with God. You were born by His purpose and for His purpose"* ('The Purpose Driven Life,' p. 17). I term this "Kingdom purpose."

- Kingdom purpose being, preordained purpose
- Kingdom purpose being, intentional divine purpose
- Kingdom purpose being, purpose, which comes from God, is commissioned and equipped by God, given sanction by God, whose steps are ordered by God, and purpose, which in turn brings glory to God.

Know that you can find success in the world and still miss your reason for being here. In other words, you can become rich and still miss out. You can become famous and still miss out. You can gain a multiplicity of degrees and still miss out. You can have great success in the corporate realm and still have no lasting purpose beyond your career, college days, having wealth, and the short seasons of celebrity, privilege, titles and rank.

Many of us even think that our value is measured by our valuables, and so we upgrade our stuff to elevate our importance, but let me serve notice that, you can drive a fancy car, eat expensive food, wear pricey clothes and own a beautiful home, and still find a void in your soul and emptiness in your heart. Why, because a car is not Christ, and a steak is not the Word of God, and our clothes are not the Holy Ghost and our house dwellings are not the Church. If the truth be told, we are here because of God. God made us for Himself. God created us to be in fellowship with Him. God formed us from the dust of the earth for His pleasure and He shaped us for His will. This was not done to stroke our ego, pad our pockets or to enlarge our territory, but God did it for the purpose of advancing His Kingdom, glorifying His Name, promoting His cause and exalting His Son. Colossians 1:16 declares: **"For by Him were all things created, that are in Heaven, and that are in earth, visible and invisible, whether they be thrones, or dominions, or principalities, or powers: all things were created by Him, and for Him."** And even Jesus, whom all things were made for found His purpose in the purpose of the Kingdom. At the age of 12 Jesus declares: **"I must be about My Father's business"** (Luke 2:49) and in John 9:4 He states: **"I must work the works of Him that sent Me, while it is day: the night cometh, when no man can work."**

Kingdom purpose is just that, it is the *purpose of the Kingdom*. It is a divinely approved walk and talk. It is mission by commission and assignment by commandment. *Kingdom purpose* is more than church membership. It is more than pew occupation. It is more than song and dance, and it is more than a feel-good moment on Sundays. *Kingdom purpose* is ministry. It is feeding the hungry, clothing the naked, providing shelter and support, aiding the blind to see and the lame to walk, lending a helping hand, showing love and being friendly, giving and forgiving, sharing and caring, standing up for justice and declaring the purpose of God.

Kingdom purpose is Kingdom passion. *Kingdom purpose* is Kingdom focus. *Kingdom purpose* is Kingdom commitment and *Kingdom purpose* is Kingdom priority. It is seeking first God's Kingdom, making Kingdom investments, striving for Kingdom greatness on Kingdom terms and pledging our allegiance to the Cross. And Kingdom children live in *Kingdom purpose.*

When you live in *Kingdom purpose*, you live in Kingdom joy, Kingdom peace, Kingdom hope and Kingdom life. And there's no life like Kingdom life. There's no joy like Kingdom joy. There's no peace like Kingdom peace and there's no hope like Kingdom hope. Kingdom life is eternal life. Kingdom joy is everlasting joy. Kingdom peace is endless peace and Kingdom hope is guaranteed. The songwriter (Edward Mote) says: *"My hope is built on nothing less, than Jesus' blood and righteousness. I dare not trust the sweetest frame, but wholly trust in Jesus' Name."* "On Christ, the solid Rock I stand, all other grounds is sinking sand."

If you want to hear Jesus say "Servant, well done," then you must walk, talk, live and give in *Kingdom purpose*. Nothing matters more and no purpose is truly purpose unless that purpose is *Kingdom purpose.*

AND THIS GOSPEL OF THE
KINGDOM SHALL BE PREACHED IN
ALL THE WORLD FOR A WITNESS
UNTO ALL NATIONS; AND THEN
SHALL THE END COME.
(MATTHEW 24:14)

Jesus of Nazareth

CHAPTER 8: SERMON EIGHT

KINGDOM ATTITUDES

(FIRST PREACHED - TRUE FOUNDATION TRANSFORMATION CHURCH — 5/11/08)

MATTHEW 5:3-12
(NIV)

"Blessed are the poor in spirit, for theirs is the Kingdom of Heaven. (4) Blessed are those who mourn, for they will be comforted. 5) Blessed are the meek, for they will inherit the earth. (6) Blessed are those who hunger and thirst for righteousness, for they will be filled. (7) Blessed are the merciful, for they will be shown mercy. (8) Blessed are the pure in heart, for they will see God. (9) Blessed are the peacemakers, for they will be called sons of God. (10) Blessed are those who are persecuted because of righteousness, for theirs is the Kingdom of Heaven. (11) Blessed are you when people insult you, persecute you and falsely say all kinds of evil against you because of Me. (12) Rejoice and be glad, because great is your reward in Heaven, for in the same way they persecuted the prophets who were before you."

The text before us is more commonly known as "the Beatitudes." They are given such designation because they give expression to the type of qualities of thought expected of those, who deem themselves *Kingdom citizens*, *followers of Christ* or *believers in God*. These are they who long for a life of true happiness and divine blessings during the stay of life here on earth and beyond life in Heaven.

The word "beatitude" is derived from the Latin term "beatus," which simply means "blessed" or "happy." This is an appropriate phrase attached to this text because, the bulk of the text begins with the word "blessed."

- Blessed are the poor in spirit (v. 3)
- Blessed are those who mourn (v. 4)
- Blessed are the meek (v. 5)
- Blessed are those who hunger and thirst for righteousness (v. 6)
- Blessed are the merciful (v. 7)
- Blessed are the pure in heart (v. 8)
- Blessed are the peacemakers (v. 9)
- Blessed are those who are persecuted because of righteousness (v. 10)
- Blessed are you when people insult you, persecute you and falsely say all kinds of evil against you because of Me (v. 11)

'Beatitude' is a declaration of promised future blessing because of some present virtue or good deed that finds origin within the framework of the mind, and as such, some people call these the "beautiful attitudes" or the "attractive attitudes." These are attitudes that dominate the way in which Jesus Himself acted and reacted while in life and ministry here on earth – attitudes that are representative of the **"new creation in Christ"** – attitudes, which reflect a desire to please and obey God, give good diplomacy to God – attitudes not so much to make happiness a life goal, but to pursue God-in-Christ as the goal and ambition for both life and joy.

You do know that if you go through life seeking happiness that it can be lost in frustration, disappointment, heartbreak and heartache, unexpected misfortunes, and in an endless quest for something better than what you currently have. And as such, you never reach a level of contentment, tranquility in life, satisfaction or of true peace in life. The Apostle Paul declares in Philippians 4:11: **"I have learned, in whatsoever state I am, therewith to be content."** However, the pursuit of happiness has led many of us to flutter from one spouse to another, or to cheat and steal in efforts to become rich, or to ingest drugs and drink alcohol in an attempt to feel good, or to chase pleasure in all the wrong places, just to escape the discontent of the world or to escalate our search to be happy and at ease within this world.

I know that written within the Declaration of Independence, along with "life" and "liberty" is named the "pursuit of happiness;" however, in contrast to the words and affirmation of our founding fathers, Jesus never sought personal happiness as a goal. His ambition was to fulfill the Will of God for His life and to do what the Father had commissioned Him to do – to say what the Father had given Him to say – to go where the Father had willed Him to go. The Bible states in Philippians 2:5 (NIV): **"Our attitude should be the same as Christ,"** who not only teaches us the "beatitudes" but also modeled them in word and deed, action and reaction, and in disposition and deliberation.

Jesus was meek and lowly, who wept for the plight of sinners. He hungered for the Word and Will of God, and Jesus showed mercy from a pure heart. He made peace between us and God, endured persecution for the sake of righteousness, demonstrated the virtues that bring true happiness, showed us that satisfaction comes from giving and not getting, and from self-denial instead of self-extravagance and self-centeredness. In essence, Jesus illustrated that contentment comes from "who we are" on the inside and not from "what we have" on the outside. In Luke 12:15 He states: **"a man's life does not consist in the abundance of his possessions."** Translation: *it's an inside thing, and if ever you desire to be happy, attitude is critical.* As a matter of fact, one of the most important qualities in life is *attitude*, for it is *attitude*, which drives behavior, and *attitude*, which determines the affect and impact that people and situations may have upon us.

Know that, the control center of our lives is our attitude and no one is in control of our control center but us. In this, we have choice, and in this, we have option, selection, preference and alternative. Daily we choose our state of being and personal actions, as well as reactions by the selection of the attitude we adopt within our minds regarding what people say to us or say about us, and as it relates to what may befall us that is common within life, such as: sickness, disappointment, opposition, tragedy, misfortune, heartbreak, and death. These are all widespread and universal, impartial and unbiased. In other words, none of us are exempt and all of us, between birth and the grave, will have to deal with some form of life difficulty and dissatisfaction, or some unwelcome or unexpected seasons of grief and challenge, tear-stained eyes and mournful cries, for such is life. Job said: **"Man that is born of a woman is of few days, and full of trouble"** (Job 14:1), but it is attitude, which settles how we handle what we face from day-to-day and over the course of a lifetime.

What *attitude* does is that, it allows us to condition our own responses, shape our own days, and coordinate our own moods, way of conduct, emotion, disposition and reply. In any given normal situation, there is nothing or nobody, which compels us to react in one way or another apart from that, which is given life by the attitude we assume. Proverbs 23:7 proclaims: **"For as he thinketh in his heart, so is he."** In other words, if we feel angry about something that happens to us or around us, that's how we choose to feel. There is nothing in the event itself, which makes it absolutely necessary for us to feel anger, bitterness, irritation, resentment or rage. It's our choice in how we feel and it's our choice in what we become because of how we feel.

Attitudes are positive, negative or neutral views of an 'attitude object,' such as: a person, event, situation, or performance, and the approach we take within the fabric of our thoughts are the advance we make within our walk, talk, feedback and temperament. No one concludes this but us, for we have choice in our thoughts. Think positively, you respond in positive ways. Think negatively, you respond in negative ways. Think neutrally and you respond in a neutral manner. Whatever the framework of the mind becomes the structure of ones life.

Attitude shapes atmosphere. *Attitude* determines altitude. *Attitude* molds character and it is attitude, which propels us into a realm of success. Oftentimes, it is not opportunity or the lack thereof that restricts us, but it's a deficiency in attitude. If you think you can't, you probably will not. *"Winners never quit and quitters never win."* I have an inspirational stone in my office, which reads: *"In the middle of difficulty lies opportunity,"* yet the visualization of such depends on what we see in our mind.

Charles Swindoll said: *"Attitude is more important than facts, more important than the past, more important than education, more important than money, than circumstances, than failures, successes, or what other people think, say, or do. It is more important than appearance, more important than giftedness, and more important than skill. It will make or break a company, a church, and a home."*

Never underestimate or miscalculate the power of 'attitude.' *Attitude* is contagious, be it good, bad, nice, nasty, positive or negative. *Attitude* has clout. It has muscle. It has influence, impact, power and persuasion, and the more optimistic the attitude, the more productive its results. Per proven facts, *attitude* can add years to ones life and good health to the body or it can reduce longevity and make one sick. Jesus teaches us that, the right attitude can make us happy and the beneficiaries of Kingdom blessings.

- Blessed are the poor in spirit, for theirs is the Kingdom of Heaven (v. 3)
- Blessed are those who mourn, for they will be comforted (v. 4)

- Blessed are the meek, for they will inherit the earth (v. 5)
- Blessed are those who hunger and thirst for righteousness, for they will be filled (v. 6)
- Blessed are the merciful, for they will be shown mercy (v. 7)
- Blessed are the pure in heart, for they will see God v. 8)
- Blessed are the peacemakers, for they will be called sons of God (v. 9)
- Blessed are those who are persecuted because of righteousness, for theirs is the Kingdom of Heaven (v. 10)
- Blessed are you when people insult you, persecute you and falsely say all kinds of evil against you because of Me (v. 11)
- Rejoice and be glad, because great is your reward in Heaven, for in the same way they persecuted the prophets who were before you (v. 12)

True happiness comes from looking at life from God's perspective and from adopting the right attitude, which synchronizes with God's. The question remains: *are you in sync with God?*

Happiness is not by chance but it's a matter of choice, and the choice must begin with the attitudes we take and with the attitudes we make. It's not a matter of what happens to us, but it's all a matter of our reaction to what happens to us or around us. **"Let this mind be in you, which was also in Christ Jesus"** (Philippians 2:5).

Before you say a word, check your attitude and before you do another deed, check your attitude.

- Are you humble and repentant?
- Are you teachable and godly sorrowful?
- Are you hungry for the Word and thirsty to do justice?
- Are you merciful and of a clean heart, and do you make peace or raise hell?

It's an attitude thing, which pleases God and it's an attitude thing that gains blessings. Happiness, peace and joy are a matter of attitude. If you want to enjoy life to its fullest, guard the way you think and you chart your course in life.

LET THE DEAD BURY THEIR DEAD:
BUT GO THOU AND PREACH
THE KINGDOM OF GOD.
(LUKE 9:60)

Jesus of Nazareth

CHAPTER 9: SERMON NINE

KINGDOM CHARACTERISTICS

(FIRST PREACHED - TRUE FOUNDATION TRANSFORMATION CHURCH — 5/25/08)

JOHN 13:34-35

"A new commandment I give unto you, that ye love one another; as I have loved you, that ye also love one another. (35) By this shall all men know that ye are My disciples, if ye have love one to another."

The term "characteristic" is defined as *"a distinguishing trait, feature, or quality."* It is a unique aspect of something or someone that helps to identify us, to set us apart, or that, which describes and differentiates an individual, group of people, or things from those and that, which are similar to it or of its own kind.

A *characteristic* is much like a *trademark*, in that, as in business affairs a name or symbol or the combination of the two are used to identify a product or artifact and to give it proprietary status, so is a trademark also *"a distinctive characteristic by which a person or thing has come to be known,"* such as certain mannerisms or gestures, facial makeup and movements, words spoken or perhaps, words not spoken – a smile, a frown, a birthmark or defect – a hairstyle or mode of dress, or even a talent, gift, or a trademark of deed or the lack thereof. You know some people are known for what they do and some for what they don't do.

In seeking to solve crimes or to pinpoint the perpetrators of crimes, law enforcement agents often inquire from eyewitnesses about the physical attributes or peculiarities of individuals that are considered suspect to a crime. Such inquiries are simply questions about characteristics: how tall, what color, any outstanding features, all of which are designed to assist law enforcement in the apprehension of someone that may be at fault of committing or abetting in the crime or crimes investigated. Some characteristics are exclusive to us, such as our fingerprints and DNA. Our fingerprints are unique to us and DNA provides genetic information about us that is carried beyond us from one generation to the next that can identify who we belong to and who it is that belongs to us.

As it pertains to our text, Jesus highlights an element of character that I call *"Kingdom DNA,"* which ties us to Him and yokes us with the Kingdom, without which, the Apostle Paul in the Thirteenth Chapter of the 1st Book of Corinthians declares, all that is said and done is but **"a resounding gong or a clanging cymbal"** (v. 1). In other words, it's but 'noise with no distinction' and 'volume without meaning' if what we say and do are not intermingled with the dominate Kingdom characteristic of "love." Scripture gives us others, such as: *joy, peace, patience, kindness, goodness, faithfulness, gentleness,* and *self-control,* along with *forgiveness, humility,* and *compassion,* and even more. All of these are empowered and given life by the main characteristic of *love.* **"And now abideth faith, hope and love, but the greatest of these is love"** (1 Corinthians 13:13).

Love is the *end-all* and *be-all* of Christianity. It is the prevailing factor, which can conquer hatred and cast out fear, overcome evil and endure throughout both time and eternity. Two things will stand when all else fails – the *Word of God* and *love.* And one of the main purposes of the church is to manifest to the world God's form of love, which is unlike the love of the world: selfish, self-seeking, self-centered and conditional. In contrast, God's love is unselfish, self-giving love and self-denying. It is stereotypical and emblematic of Jesus Christ Himself, who patterned, in the flesh, this very love for us to follow. And it is Jesus, who in our text, equates such characteristic as representative of Himself and describes for us, what distinguishes us as true disciples of His and citizens of God's Kingdom: **"A new commandment I give unto you, that ye love one another; as I have loved you, that ye also love one another. By this shall all men know that ye are My disciples, if ye have love one to another."** In this it is interesting that Jesus does not lift up many of the things that we tend to lift up to substantiate our love for Him and/or our love for each other.

It is in the words of our text, where Jesus defines for us the type of love He expects of us, and it is in the words of our text, where Jesus demands of us that we demonstrate such love that He defines for us toward each other. In the Greek it's called *"Agape,"* and *agape* is a love, which actions are always for the benefit of someone else. It is one-way giving and one-way sacrifice, and it does what it does without expectation of reciprocation.

To love *agape*-style means that you **1)** see a need and move to meet that need, **2)** take no thought of personal cost, **3)** you don't consider whether or not the person deserves to have the need met, **4)** you don't consider what you will get out of it when you help somebody or do good on the behalf of someone else, and **5)** you make your decisions and do what you do always for the welfare of the other person. In this, it is never about us and always about them. And in order to underscore this understanding of love further Jesus inserts the clause into His text, **"as I have loved you."**

"As I have loved you" brings clarification to the command and invalidation to ignorance. The disciples were to treat each other as Jesus had treated them. In essence, this is the way God wants us to conduct ourselves. As God is toward us, so He expects from us. In other words, as God is patient with us, so we ought to be patient with one another. In other words, as God is merciful toward us, so we should be merciful toward each other. In other words, as God is forgiving of us, so we, in like manner, ought to forgive one other. In other words, as God has been gracious toward us, so we ought to extend grace to each other. I often say, *what flows to us should flow from us.* This is the way of the Godhead and how we ought to reflect the Kingdom in our dealings with one another.

Jesus did not say that they shall know us by our name or by the name on our buildings, but by our **"love one to another."** We all are aware that it's one thing to be called a "Christian" and yet another to demonstrate the ways of Christ. We are aware too that it's one thing to have the Name of Christ written on our church signs and still another for Christ to be on the inside, in fellowship with us and us with Him. In other words, it's not in what we call ourselves, but it's all in how we treat each other, and in how we communicate to one another, and in how we defend each other, encourage one another, build up each other and are a support system to one another.

The world around us will not identify us with Jesus if they see us fighting with each other, holding grudges against one another, refusing to speak to each other, not forgiving one another; if they hear us gossiping about one another, condemning each other, lying on one another or perhaps, backstabbing each other. As a matter of fact, it is possible that, the reason people outside of the church are reluctant to come into the church is due to the fact of how we conduct ourselves as the church. In many instances, is no different than what the world sees and hears at home and in the streets.

Why leave fussing and fighting at home to come to church to fuss and fight, or why seek refuge from hell in hell? Gandhi once said, *"I would be a Christian if it were not for Christians."* I'm not talking about nobody, just quoting what he said. In many ways, we are our worst enemies, and instead of representing Christ, we become embarrassments to the Kingdom when we conduct ourselves unlike Christ – when we are unloving, uncaring, unforgiving, and unrepentant. Jesus said: **"By this shall all men know that ye are My disciples, if ye have love one to another."**

In one sense, when Jesus says: **"A new commandment I give unto you,"** the command is not new, for as part of the Mosaic law was the command to **"love thy neighbor as thyself"** (Leviticus 19:18). However, some people don't love themselves, and some people will do harm to themselves, and some people don't esteem themselves very much, thus Jesus says: **"A new commandment I give unto you, that ye love one another; as I have loved you, that ye also love one another."** In this Jesus takes the standard of love to another level when He says: **"as I have loved you."** And this type of love can be summed up in one word – "sacrificial." Jesus' whole life was a life of sacrifice. He came not for Himself but for the benefit of all others.

- When He left His throne in Glory – it was about sacrifice
- When He took on the form of man – it was about sacrifice
- When He said: **"Not My will but Thine be done"** (Luke 22:42) – it was about sacrifice.
- When He gave His life on the Cross, Jesus died not for Himself or because of Himself but **"He was wounded for our transgressions, and bruised for our iniquities"** (Isaiah 53:5). Paul says: **"He made Himself of no reputation and took upon Him the form of a servant, and being made in the likeness of men, He humbled Himself, and made sacrifice unto death, even to death on a cross"** (Philippians 2:7).

In John 15:13 Jesus says: **"Greater love has no man than this that he lay down his life for his friends."** In 1ˢᵗ John Chapter 3 it is stated:

"This is how we know what love is: Jesus Christ laid down His life for us. And we ought to lay down our lives for our brothers. If anyone has material possessions and sees his brother in need but has no pity on him, how can the love of God be in him" (vv. 16-17)?

Kingdom love is about sacrifice. *Kingdom love* is about surrender. *Kingdom love* is about giving the very best that one has and denying oneself for the sake of someone else. **"For God so loved the world that He gave His One and Only Son, that whoever believes in Him shall not perish but have Eternal Life"** (John 3:16). How can we represent the Kingdom, if we have not the love of the Kingdom? The Word says: **"let us love one another, for love comes from God"** (1 John 4:7). **"God is love"** (1 John 4:8).

Love is the trademark of the Kingdom and the main attribute of discipleship. Love fulfills the Law. Love outweighs hate. Love reflects Christ and love is what we need.

We need to show love in the church. We need to take love beyond the church. We need love in our homes. We need love in our schools. We need love in our government and love is needed throughout the world. The songwriter says: *"What the world needs now is love, sweet love; it's the only thing there's too little of."*

We need family love. We need friendship love. We need Christian love and love above love. The Bible says: **"Owe no man anything but to love one another"** (Romans 13:8). I need love. You need love. We need to show love to each other. It's the God way. It's the Christian way. It is the way of Jesus Christ.

NO MAN, HAVING PUT HIS HAND TO
THE PLOW, AND LOOKING BACK, IS
FIT FOR THE KINGDOM OF GOD.
(LUKE 9:62)

Jesus of Nazareth

CHAPTER 10: SERMON TEN

KINGDOM PRIVILEGE

(FIRST PREACHED - TRUE FOUNDATION TRANSFORMATION CHURCH — 6/1/08)

MATTHEW 7:7-8
(NIV)

"Ask and it will be given to you; seek and you will find; knock and the door will be opened to you. (8) For everyone who asks receives; he who seeks finds; and to him who knocks, the door will be opened."

The term "privilege" speaks of *a special advantage or allowance that is exclusive to some and not enjoyed by all.* Some define it as *"a right reserved,"* or as a *"benefit granted,"* or as an opportunity to do something or obtain something, which most people never have the chance to do or have.

A "privilege" is also seen as something that is inherited from one generation to another, or something that is gained through endorsement, association, friendship or through generosity. It is also something that is viewed from the *standpoint of exemption,* or from the *angle of exoneration,* or from the perspective of being excluded from deserved penalty, punishment, burden or affliction.

In one sense *privilege* is favor. It is an act of kindness, benevolence, thoughtfulness and compassion, and of exceptional consideration. In another sense, *privilege* is something that is worked toward, labored for, acquired through the accumulation of years of service or through the addition of years to age or life.

When you consider *privilege* from an earthly perspective, as noted, it can be earned; however, *Kingdom privilege*, that which flows down from Heaven is always a matter of "grace through faith." In other words, there is nothing that we can ever do to merit divine goodwill apart from our acknowledgment of who God is and recognition of what God can do. Without God we are nothing, can claim nothing and have no deeds or ownership of nothing. With God nothing is out of our reach, beyond our grasp, above our petition or too hard for God to supply. As a matter of fact Jesus states in Luke 12:32: **"Fear not, little flock; for it is your Father's good pleasure to give you the Kingdom."** In other words, blessing those who belong to Him delights God, and giving to us who call upon His Name *in faith* brings satisfaction and enjoyment to God.

In Matthew 7:11 Jesus declares: **"If ye then, being evil, know how to give good gifts unto your children, how much more shall your Father which is in Heaven give good things to them that ask Him?"** But as this text and our chosen text invokes, we cannot expect without 'asking.' *Asking* is the first criteria of anticipation, and to substantiate this point the writer of the Book of James adds: **"we have not because we ask not"** (James 4:2). In addition, *asking* must always be done in faith. The Word says: **"Without faith, it is impossible to please Him, for he who comes to God must believe that God is, and that He is a rewarder of them that diligently seek Him"** (Hebrews 11:6). The term *diligently* means, *to give careful and meticulous effort to obtain.* It involves consistency. It entails perseverance. It engages determination and it mandates that one would have a made-up mind.

Spiritually speaking, the *diligent seeker* will go to any length to find God, and to obey His Word, and to obtain His favor, and to honor His Name. Like Jacob wrestled with an Angel of the LORD until the breaking of the day and would not let go without a blessing from the LORD. Like Abraham received Word from the LORD and began a walk of faith, leaving his country and kindred to go toward a land simply promised by God. Like Zacchaeus, who did not allow crowd or height to impede him from getting a glimpse of or audience with Jesus. Like Job, who lost all that he had, yet he maintained his trust in God declaring: **"though He slay me, yet will I trust in Him"** (Job 13:15). **"As the deer panteth after the water brooks"** (Psalm 42:1), so goes the soul of them that seek God.

The 'diligent seeker' is not someone who rarely reads the Bible nor someone who barely attends church, nor someone that seldom finds time to pray, nor someone whose faith wavers like the wave of the sea is driven with the wind and tossed. No, the *diligent seeker* is a steady Bible reading. The diligent seeker believes in what he or she has read. The *diligent seeker* practices what he or she believes, and the *diligent seeker* makes time to pray and can be found in the Lord's House 'in their rightful place.' These are they, who take God at His Word. They don't quit. They don't give up. They don't throw in the towel or resign after "asking," "seeking," and "knocking," and nothing seems to happen.

The Greek tense of our text does not simply mean to, "ask, seek, and knock" one time, but to *"keep on asking,"* and to *"keep on seeking,"* and to *"keep on knocking,"* with all diligence and devotion. It is not just emphasizing activity, or mere words, or movement and gestures, but persistence. Some things only come through persistence.

You do remember, in Luke 18, that Jesus gave us a parable about a widow and an unjust judge, who, at first was denied what she asked for, but who, because of her persistence, was granted all that she requested by the same one, who denied her in the beginning. In seeking a job you need to be persistent. In seeking help you need to be persistent. If you want to grow in your relationship with God you need to be persistent. Whatever you desire in life to attain, you need to be persistent.

Understand that, even though God knows our every need and has knowledge of our every desire, God still wants us to "ask." God still wants us to petition Him. God still wants us to pray, to "seek His face," to "inquire in His Temple," and to make our requests known unto Him. It is through "asking," "seeking" and "knocking" that we display our faith in God, and demonstrate our dependence on God, and exhibit our hopes through God, and showcase that we appreciate who God is and what He is able to do. And the key again is to "ask." Put together the first letters of "**a**sk," "**s**eek," and "**k**nock," and you have **ASK**. Add to this the fact that, we must ask without doubt, waver, suspicion or trembling. No matter what the obstacle or complication, God wants us to "ask."

Concerning Abraham, Paul says that: **"He staggered not at the promise of God through unbelief; but was strong in faith, giving glory to God; and being fully persuaded that, what God had promised, He was able also to perform"** (Romans 4:20-21). Like him, you've got to know that God is able and you cannot be afraid to ask Him. Don't listen to the naysayers or pay attention to the individuals that would tell you that it cannot be done. Always bear in mind what Jesus says: **"ask, and it shall be given to you; seek, and ye shall find; knock and the door will be opened to you."**

Let me also say that, "Kingdom privilege" is *privilege* in the sense of favor. We cannot force God's Hand, like some people teach us, and we cannot manipulate Heaven, like some people preach to us. How can we, who are sinners, saved by grace demand anything of God? How can we command anything from God? How can we insist that God owes us, and that God is obligated to us, and that God must do what we maintain He must do? *But God*, in His mercy, and God, through His grace, and God, because He is kind, caring, thoughtful and sympathetic of what we go through, and of our needs, and of our desires within life, stands ready to grant us all things. Jesus says, **"But seek ye first the Kingdom of God, and His righteousness; and all these things shall be added unto you"** (Matthew 6:33).

One of the tragedies of our Christian faith lies in the weakness of our Christian faith. We, who claim God as Father, fall short in our belief of what God can do. We tend to forget the tremendous privileges that are ours as children of the Kingdom. Does not the Bible teach us that **"the wealth of the wicked is laid up for the righteous"** (Proverbs 13:22)? Is it not written and recorded that **"no good thing will God withhold from them, who walk uprightly before Him"** (Psalm 84:11)? Can you not read in His Word that, God has a place for His people, and that God takes care of His own, and that **"the earth is the LORD's and the fulness thereof, this world and they that dwell therein"** (Psalm 24:1), and that all things belong to Him?

There are but three words that can unlock the greatest treasures of the universe: ask, seek and knock. Jesus said: "Ask, seek, and knock," and you can have what you ask for, and you can find what you're looking for, and you can enjoy the right of passage into the realm of God's provisions.

Scripture declares: **"God is able to do exceeding, abundantly; above all we ask or think"** (Ephesians 3:20). How many know that **"eye have not seen and ear have not heard"** (1 Corinthians 2:9)? God's got some stuff in storage for those that love Him. Though it rains on the just and the unjust, as a child of the King, there is *privilege* in our sonship. There is power in our relationship. There are benefits to behold and opportunities to explore. But we must speak up and make it known what we are seeking from the Lord.

In the package of salvation is the privilege of adoption. We're in the family now, and there is no joy like family joy. There is no peace like family peace. There is no hope like family hope. There is no life like family life. As a matter fact, the greatest *privilege* of our *privilege* is the *privilege* of Eternal Life. **"For God so loved the world, that He gave His Only Begotten Son, that whosoever believeth in Him, should not perish but have Everlasting Life"** (John 3:16).

EPILOGUE

*"If ye then be risen with Christ, seek those things which are
above, where Christ sitteth on the right hand of God. Set your
affection on things above, not on things on the earth.*
(COLOSSIANS 3:1-2)

I pray that the contents of this book have propelled you to a greater
commitment to Kingdom purpose, priority, investment and focus. For
the believer in Christ, our discipleship is *followship*, and by *followship* I
mean; we must dedicate ourselves to walking in the footsteps of Jesus (1
Peter 2:21). For Jesus, the Kingdom agenda was His only agenda. He
had no other. His testimonies were: *"My meat is to do the will of Him that
sent Me and to finish His work"* (John 4:34) and *"I must work the works of
Him that sent Me"* (John 9:4), among others. He taught us to pray, *"Thy
Kingdom come"* and *"Thy will be done."* And what greater privilege is there
in life than to be used of God as a container and instrument of His Word
and Will.

Let the 'Kingdom Word' marinate in your heart, stir up your soul,
quicken your spirit, and motivate you to 'flesh out' before the world the
light and life of Jesus Christ. Do not be ashamed of the Gospel, for truly
"it is the power of God unto salvation to every one that believes" (Romans
1:16). Do not be ashamed of your Christianity. Remember Jesus said,
*"Whosoever shall be ashamed of Me and of My words, of him shall the Son of
man be ashamed, when He shall come in His own glory, and in His Father's,
and of the holy angels"* (Luke 9:26). Do not be ashamed of testifying, while
in this world, that *it's all about the Kingdom*! For those who are faithful

to this cause, there are rewards laid up in Heaven, and to those who invite others into the circle of faith Jesus will say: *"Servant, well done!"*

This is an epilogue to this volume, but the volumes will continue. And when my volumes are completed, I pray that you will add more seed to the sermons that are yet to be preached – *"Faith cometh by hearing, and hearing by the Word of God"* (Romans 10:17). As I've sown into you, in like manner, be a sower of Kingdom things into the lives of many others. I wish you – God speed.

AFTERWORD

It has been my great pleasure knowing and interacting with the Brookins' Family, especially the patriarch, Rev. Dr. C.L. Brookins, whom I've known for many of years. It is also good to see that the educational and spiritual values that the father possessed have been passed down to this son, Rev. Dr. Larry A. Brookins.

These sermons contain solid doctrinal–foundational–spiritual principles and truths, and they can be used to persuade sinners to regeneration, saints to encouragement and backsliders to repentance. Each 'Kingdom' principle in these sermons have been well thought out and explained in such a simple manner that even a fool should not err. I like the fact that each principle is taken directly from the teachings of Jesus Christ our Lord. He was the Master Teacher, and we would do well to make His words our model, as you, Rev. Dr. Larry A. Brookins, have so eloquently done. I also like the fact that you made a clear distinction between the 'Kingdom' and the 'Church,' but yet you showed how they relate and interconnect to each other.

My prayer is that everyone who reads this book will grasp the true meaning of the 'Kingdom of God' and will model it in their churches. I also pray that God will abundantly bless you in this endeavor and all that you do to promote the 'Kingdom of God.' May He bless you *real, real, good.*

Dr. Clay Evans
Founder & Pastor Emeritus, 'Fellowship Missionary Baptist Church'

Thank you Dr. Clay Evans

   To you I extend my utmost gratitude for taking the time to review the manuscript of this book, and for adding to it your comments and insights. I do not take this lightly, but count it an honor that I am able to have you a part of this project. I will forever treasure this privilege, as well as the mark of distinction your great name adds to my endeavor to further the spread of the Gospel and edify the Body of Christ in written form. Again, I am appreciative and I am humbled, and as you've expressed to many of us down through the years, I now express to you: *may the Lord bless you, real, real, good.*

   Your Spiritual Grandson in the Ministry,

Rev. Dr. Larry A. Brookins

BONUS SERMON:

THE STRUGGLES OF KINGDOM LIVING

(FIRST PREACHED - TRUE FOUNDATION TRANSFORMATION CHURCH — 7/19/09)

ROMANS 7:14-25
(NIV)

"We know that the Law is spiritual; but I am unspiritual, sold as a slave to sin. (15) I do not understand what I do. For what I want to do I do not do, but what I hate I do. (16) And if I do what I do not want to do, I agree that the Law is good. (17) As it is, it is no longer I myself who do it, but it is sin living in me. (18) I know that nothing good lives in me, that is, in my sinful nature, for I have the desire to do what is good, but I cannot carry it out. (19) For what I do is not the good I want to do; no, the evil I do not want to do--this I keep on doing. (20) Now if I do what I do not want to do, it is no longer I who do it, but it is sin living in me that does it. (21) So I find this law at work: When I want to do good, evil is right there with me. (22) For in my inner being I delight in God's law; (23) but I see another law at work in the members of my body, waging war against the law of my mind and making me a prisoner of the law of sin at work within my members. (24) What a wretched man I am! Who will rescue me from this body of death? (25) Thanks be to

God--through Jesus Christ our Lord! So then, I myself in my mind am a slave to God's law, but in the sinful nature a slave to the law of sin."

The 7th Chapter of the Book of Romans addresses a common conflict of the Christian life. The writer himself admits to this conflict within his own life and he pens an autobiographical sketch of his personal struggles within himself, which is also the experience and assessment for all of us.

Our writer is the Apostle Paul, and Paul was not just having a bad day when he writes the contents of this chapter, nor was he suffering from a sense of inadequacy and low self-esteem. In the verses of our text, Paul takes a long, hard look at his deepest and darkness inner self, and what he sees in himself and of himself is somewhat troubling to himself, but true. Although Paul's aspiration was to live for God and do what was right at all times, in reality, like all of us, there were times, Paul acknowledges, where he found himself in failure to carry out the considerations of God's Law. Though in the opening verses of this chapter Paul examines the Law and pronounces the Law good, like all of us, who are on the salvation side of the Cross of Christ, Paul struggled to keep the commandments of God, and Paul wrestled with opposing desires within himself. There was one desire to please God and another desire to please himself, for what resided within Paul is what resides within every born-again believer.

There are two sides to all of us, one innately good and the other instinctively evil – one righteous and one unrighteous – one decent and one not so decent.

One side of us can be nice, and the other side can be unpleasant. One side of us can love, the other side can hate. One side of us can speak well of people, while the other has nothing good to say about anybody. And before you pat yourself on the back and put down someone else, let me say that, none of us are perfect. We all have issues. We all have mood swings. We all have a different us and we all have imperfections.

As Christians, Scripture teaches us that we are to strive toward perfection, which is still the goal in Christian growth, but the truth of the matter is; we shall not reach perfection in this life, especially in this body of clay, filth, corruption and carnality. The body of this flesh has no morals or proclivity for perfection. It does not care what it does. It does not care who it hurts. It does not care how it obtains what it is it obtains. It simply wants to feed itself what self wants and to have what self wants when self desires to have what self wants. The truth of the matter is, the flesh does not even care about itself. It craves harmful matters to itself like cigarettes and drugs, and the more it feeds itself these addictive elements, the more the elements take over to enhance the flesh's cravings – that's why it's difficult for you to break the habit and quit.

Within the context of our text Paul confesses: **"For I know that in me (that is, in my flesh,) dwelleth no good thing"** (v. 18), and what he confesses about his flesh also applies to our flesh. Our *flesh is a mess*. And because the *flesh is a mess*, it needs to be controlled by a mind or by a spirit that is given over to the will of God, for if the mind or spirit is not directed by the will of God, than it simply allows the flesh to have its own way – that's why the psalmist says: **"Thy word have I hid in my heart, that I might not sin against Thee"** (Psalm 119:11). Those who are *in the flesh* or those who are ruled by the physical desires of the human body—cannot and will not ever, in such state please God, that's what Romans 8:8 says: **"So then they that are in the flesh cannot please God."**

Within each new life of regeneration there are two natures: one nature is *sinful* and the other nature is *spiritual*, and the sin nature within us is constantly at war against the new nature of the spirit. The inclination of the sin nature is the law of the flesh, but the inclination of the spirit nature is the law of God. And this same Paul says in Galatians 5:17 that: **"the flesh lusteth against the spirit."** In other words, the sin nature embraces and has an appetite for sinful things, while the spirit nature craves and pursues the righteous things of God. They are in competition with each other and diametrically opposed to one another. And though as Christians our intent is not to allow our physical desires to rule us, sometimes they do. Sometimes we eat more than we want to eat and sometimes we drink more than we want to drink. And while many of us, if not most of us want to do what God commands of us to do, if we but be honest, sometimes we don't. The Bible says: **"Let a man examine himself"** (1 Corinthians 11:28). Sometimes we allow our flesh to have its way and we end up in a place or position that is unchristian, corrupt, unfamiliar, or devastating.

Sometimes we contemplate the good but we execute the bad. Sometimes we purpose the moral but we perform the immoral. Sometimes we intend the right but we achieve the wrong, and sometimes we strategize a correct procedure, but we error in the process.

Many of us have good intentions but bad results, and we find ourselves confused, bewildered, perplexed and baffled by some things we end up doing. But, we're not alone. Paul says: **"I do not understand what I do. For what I want to do I do not do, but what I hate I do"** (v. 15). This is the struggle of Kingdom living. Greater than the external struggles we face with finances and in relationships, is the internal struggles within ourselves.

Have you ever chided yourself? Have you ever reprimanded yourself? You did something you shouldn't have done, and it was not because you didn't know better—you knew better, but you just didn't follow through. Something got the best of you. Something altered your plans and agenda. Something steered you off course and caused you to do the opposite of what you set out to do. Some things you said you'll never do again, but you find yourself doing them again, and again, and again, and again. In spite of the fact that you're saved now and in spite of the fact that, in your heart you truly do love Jesus—sometimes you find yourself in a struggle. Sometimes you feel a tug of war going on within you.

Something is pulling you one way and something is pulling you another way. You're Christian—yes. You're devoted to the Lord—yes. You want to do what God wants you to do—yes, but sometimes you even let yourself down. Sometimes, you get disgusted with yourself. Sometimes, you become appalled at yourself, and sometimes you make your own self sick.

Have you ever asked yourself: *what's going on?* Why did I do what I did? Why did I say what I said? Why did I go where I went? What's wrong with me? What's gotten into me? Tell your neighbor: *'you're not crazy'* —*'you're not by yourself'* —*'there's simply two of you in you.'* There's the spirit and the flesh, the mind and the body, the inward man and the outward man, and there's the good you and the bad you. Don't panic. It's common. They are one and the same.

Though we've surrendered ourselves to God, we are still made of flesh and the offsprings of sin, and thereby, we are still exposed to the sin nature of our flesh, and the sin nature naturally leans away from God and towards sin. Yet, sin beckons us in order to bind us and enslave us, so that we do things that the spirit side of us is not inclined to do—so that we do things outside of the will of God—so that we do things that after we've done what we do, we regret what we've done.

Have you ever done something that you wish you've never done? Have you ever been somewhere that you wish you've never gone? Have you ever said something that you wish you've never said, and have you ever found yourself in a struggle with yourself? Guess what, you're not alone. We all have this dilemma. We all have this problem. We are all torn at times. The struggle is not unique and the difficulty is universal. Scripture says: **"All have sinned and come short of God's glory"** (Romans 3:23). Scripture says: **"There is none righteous, no, not one"** (Romans 3:10). And if someone tells you that since they've accepted Jesus into their life they've sinned no more—they're lying, and lying is a sin. Everybody, everyday, still needs God's grace. Look at somebody and tell them: *'I'm in the struggle.' I need help. I need deliverance. I need rescue. I can't do this by myself.*

In Romans Chapter 6 Paul pictures the process of becoming a Christian as *death* and *resurrection*. It is here where he illustrates that, a sinner dies, is buried in baptism, and then raised to walk anew in Christ within life. Death denotes separation, and thus Paul expounds that, in regeneration, the old sinner is gone and a new saint has appeared. But then in Chapter 7, as well as in our new life as Christians we discover that, the sinner we use to be is not as dead as we think. We may have eulogized the old, but the old keeps popping up. We may have poured dirt on the old, but the old keeps materializing.

In our efforts to please God and in our diligence to live the Kingdom way, the old us keeps exhuming itself from out of the grave of our past, and struggling with the new us in our present in an attempt to regain control of us, in order to once again enslave us to the will of the flesh, which is always contrary to the will of God. I'm just looking for some real folk—some people who have this same struggle of spirit and of flesh, and of right and of wrong, and of good and of evil, and of saint and sinner. I'm looking for some people who can identify with what I'm saying.

Sometimes it takes quite a struggle to keep the sinful nature or the old you subdued, under control, in check and buried. Some of you try but you still cuss. Some of you try but you still get drunk. Some of you try but you still fornicate, lie, cheat, and steal. My real folk would agree that, sometimes it becomes rather difficult to *mortify the deeds of the flesh*, and sometimes we win and sometimes we lose.

I'm not saying this to condone sin in any way, but sometimes we do the right things and sometimes we do the wrong things. Sometimes we say the right words and sometimes we say the wrong words. Sometimes we please God, but sometimes we miss the mark and please the flesh, and we must admit that it's a struggle sometimes living the Kingdom life.

It's a struggle sometimes loving people and being nice to some people. It's a struggle sometimes paying your tithe and giving God worship. It's a struggle sometimes coming to Church, and praying, and reading your Bible, and coming to Bible study, Sunday school, being faithful in your service, and being all that God would have us to be. But I've come to declare today that, the Kingdom life is worth the struggle— that it pays to live right—that it pays to serve God—that it pays to be faithful, and it pays to pray – that it pays to come to Sunday school, Bible study and Morning Worship. It pays to love. It pays to be kind. It pays to be nice and it pays to live life on God's terms. The Bible says: **"Be not weary in well doing, for in due season, ye shall reap if you faint not"** (Galatians 6:9).

We're in a struggle, and we can't win in our own strength, will power, or might. Some have tried and they've failed. Some have tried and they've faltered. We must acknowledge our shortcomings and then confess our sins.

In confession there is forgiveness. In confession there is victory. The Bible says: **"If we confess our sins, God is faithful and just to forgive our sins, and to cleanse us from all unrighteousness"** (1 Jon 1:9). There is a way out. We all struggle, but we can win. We all struggle, but there is help. No temptation has befallen any of us where God has not provided a way of escape. Note: 1 Corinthians 10:13

Our help is in Jesus. Our hope is in Jesus. He is the answer to every question and the solution to our problem.

With Jesus, we become righteous, and in Jesus, our sins are covered. He gives us victory and reassurance that everything will be alright.

I know it gets rough sometimes, but we can make it. I know it gets tough sometimes, but we can make it. The struggle is almost over. The Kingdom way is the best way. **"Be ye steadfast, unmovable, and always abounding in God's work, for as much as you know that your labor is not in vain in the Lord"** (1 Corinthians 15:58). Hold on just a little while longer, your help is on the way.

- **"Weeping may endure for a night, but joy comes in the morning"** (Psalm 30:5)
- **"Now unto Him that is able to keep us from falling, and to present us faultless before the presence of God's glory with exceeding joy"** (Jude 1:24).

Don't give up and don't give in. There will come a time when heartache will be no more, troubles will cease, and pain will subside. Soon, and very soon, the struggle will be over. As a matter of fact, as believers, we ought to say, in faith, *my struggle is over! This too shall pass!* **"All things work together for the good to them who love the Lord, who are the called according to His purpose"** (Romans 8:28). No pain, no gain. No cross, no crown.

SOURCES CONSULTED

Androzzo, Alma Bazel. 1945. *If I Can Help Somebody.* Made Famous by Mahalia Jackson. Public Domain.

Bonhoeffer, Dietrich. 1963. *The Cost of Discipleship.* Revised & Unabridged Edition. New York: The Macmillan Company

Holliday, Billie & Arthur Herzog, Jr. 1941. *God Bless the Child.* Words & Music by Billie Holliday & Arthur Herzog, Jr.

Mote, Edward. 1836. *My Hope is Built.* Music: William B Bradbury. Public Domain.

Swindoll, Charles R. *Attitude.* Quote.

Warren, Rick. 2002. *The Purpose Driven Life.* Grand Rapids, Michigan: Zondervan

Wesley, Charles. 1762. *A Charge to Keep I Have.* Music: Lowell Mason, 1832. Public Domain.

Coming Soon:

"It's all about the Kingdom"
Volume Two

- Kingdom Conversation -
- Kingdom Integrity -
- Kingdom Power -
- Kingdom Pride -
- Kingdom Relationships -
- Kingdom Practice -
- Kingdom Choices -
- Kingdom Fitness -
- Kingdom Customs -
- Kingdom Peace -

• Sermons contained in this volume and future volumes also available for purchase on CD and DVD. You may inquire by calling (773) 994-8896 or visiting us on the Web at: www.tftchurch.org

• Please share your comments with me: pastorbrookins@sbcglobal.net

• If in Chicago, worship with me: True Foundation Transformation Church, 8801 South Normal Avenue Chicago, IL 60620

LaVergne, TN USA
12 February 2010
172886LV00007B/1/P